LEARNING FOR LIFE AND WORK 1

NI Key Stage 3

P. Dornan, K. Armstrong,
L. Curragh, L. McEvoy,
J. McCurdy and J. McCusker

Hodder Murray
A MEMBER OF THE HODDER HEADLINE GROUP

The Publishers would like to thank the following for permission to reproduce copyright material:

Photo credits
p.1 Purestock X; **p.4** Lisa Pines Photonica/Getty Images; **p.6** © David Pollack/Corbis; **p.7** *L* Photodisc/Photolibrary, *CL* Seth Joel/Taxi/Getty Images, *CR* Photodisc, *R* Karan Kapoor/Stone; **p.11** Hans Neleman/Stone/Getty Images; **p.13** © Schlegelmilch/Corbis; **p.20** *L & R* Purestock X; **p.21** © Hein van den Heuvel/zefa/Corbis; **p.22** Peter Glass/Alamy; **p.23** Zac Macaulay/The Image Bank/Getty Images; **p.24** Liu Xiaoyang/Alamy; **p.25** *T* © iStockphoto.com/Herbert Kratky, *B* Jan Stromm/Photonic/Getty Images; **p.26** *L* Neil Bromhall/Science Photo Library, *R* © Bob Battersby; Eye Ubiquitous/Corbis; **p.27** Chris Clinton/Taxi/Getty Images; **p.34** *L* © Brooks Kraft/Corbis, *R* Paul Loven/Photographer's Choice/Getty Images, **p.36** *T* © Silva Joao/Corbis Sygma, *C* © Bettmann/Corbis, *B* © Bohemian Nomad Picturemakers/Corbis; **p.37** UN/DPI Photo; **p.42** *TL* Boris Heger/AP/EMPICS, *BL* © Alison Wright/Corbis, *R* © Maurizio Gambarini/dpa/Corbis; **p.43** Martial Trezzini/AP/EMPICS; **p.44** © Hulton-Deutsch Collection/Corbis; **p.45** *TL* Courtesy of Lesley McEvoy, *BL* Courtesy of The Very Reverend Dr Houston McKelvey, *TR* Courtesy of the Christian Brothers, *BR* Courtesy of John McCusker; **p.46** Purestock X; **p.49** © iStockphoto.com/Ayaaz Rattansi; **p.50** © Ed Kashi/Corbis; **p.52** *T* Picture by Press Eye, *CT, CB & B* © Geray Sweeney; **p.53** *T* Courtesy of NICEM, *C* Courtesy of the Community Relations Council, *B* Courtesy of An Munia Tober; **p.56** © Bettmann/Corbis; **p.59** *T* © iStockphoto.com/Sambrogio, *C* Photodisc, *B* Chris Bacon/ PA/EMPICS; **p.60** *L* Paul Loven/Photographer's Choice/Getty Images, *C* Picture by Press Eye, *TR* © Bohemian Nomad Picturemakers/Corbis, *B* Courtesy of the Christian Brothers; **p.65** *T* Purestock X, *CT* Zubin Shrof/Taxi/Getty Images, *CB* Photofusion Picture Library/Alamy, *B* Martin Barraud/Stone+/Getty Images; **p.66** *TL* Matthew Peters/Manchester United/Getty Images, *TR* Albert Ferreira/Rex Features, *B* Richard Young/Rex Features; **p.68** *TL* Purestock X, *TR* Photodisc, *BL* Horizon International Images Limited/Alamy, *BR* Adrian Weinbrecht/The Image Bank/Getty Images; **p.69** *L* Rex Features, *C* Gareth Cattermole/Getty Images Entertainment/Getty Images, *R* Paul Faith/PA/EMPICS; **p.73** Purestock X; **p.74** David Fisher/Rex Features; **p.80** Irish Linen Centre & Lisburn Museum Photgraph; **p.82** *L* Purestock X, *R* © William Gottlieb/Corbis; **p.83** *TL* © Rykoff Collection/Corbis, *BL* Purestock X, *TC* © Corbis, *BC* Greg Williams/Rex Features, *TR* © Hulton-Deutsch Collection/Corbis, *BR* © Royalty-Free/Corbis; **p.84** *All* © Geray Sweeney; **p.85** Purestock X; **p.87** *TL* John Powell/Rex Features, *TR, BL, BR* Purestock X, *CT* Janis Christie/Photographer's Choice/Getty Images, *CB* © Royalty-Free/Corbis.

Acknowledgements
p.80 the Ulster Star for the article from the *Lisburn Echo*.

Every effort has been made to trace all copyright holders, but if any have been inadvertently overlooked the Publishers will be pleased to make the necessary arrangements at the first opportunity.

Although every effort has been made to ensure that website addresses are correct at time of going to press, Hodder Murray cannot be held responsible for the content of any website mentioned in this book. It is sometimes possible to find a relocated web page by typing in the address of the home page for a website in the URL window of your browser.

Orders: please contact Bookpoint Ltd, 130 Milton Park, Abingdon, Oxon OX14 4SB. Telephone: (44) 01235 827720. Fax: (44) 01235 400454. Lines are open 9.00–5.00, Monday to Saturday, with a 24-hour message answering service. Visit our website at www.hoddereducation.co.uk

Cover photos: Belfast City Hall, © Geray Sweeney/Corbis; Mother holding infant daughter, © Stuart Westmorland/Corbis; Teenagers talking, © Steve Skjold/Alamy.

Illustrations by Oxford Designers and Illustrators.
Design in 11pt New Century Schoolbook by Black Dog Design.
Printed in Italy.

A catalogue record for this title is available from the British Library

ISBN-13: 978 0340 927 083

CONTENTS

Education for Employability

INTRODUCTION

Hello and welcome! Learning for Life and Work's aim is to help you to achieve your potential and to make informed and responsible decisions throughout your life journey of growth and change. The purpose is to help you develop:

1 as an individual (mostly but not only through Personal Development),
2 as a contributor to society (mostly through Local and Global Citizenship),
3 as a contributor to the economy and environment (mostly through Education for Employability).

Each book in the course is divided into these three main sections and then broken down into topics. Each topic has a big question as its title to investigate. Throughout the topics you will find the following features.

Learning intentions

Each topic starts by outlining the learning intentions – these are the skills and knowledge you should be learning as you make your way through the topic.

Activities

Each topic has a number of activities. You may be asked to work as an individual, in pairs, in small groups or as a class. The activities have a structure, but because each person and group is unique, there is room for you to be unpredictable and come up with something that no one else has thought of. The activities work best when you are enthusiastic, give them a go and develop and agree some helpful ground rules for working with others. Have fun!

Thinking skills and personal capabilities

Alongside each activity there is an icon. There are five different icons in all and these signpost the main thinking skills and personal capabilities you will be developing while carrying out the activity. The following table shows which skills each icon stands for.

Skill	Icon	Description
Managing Information		Research and manage information effectively to investigate personal development, citizenship and employability issues.
Thinking, Problem Solving, Decision Making		Show deeper understanding by thinking critically and flexibly, solving problems and making informed decisions.
Being Creative		Demonstrate creativity and initiative when developing ideas and following them through.
Working with Others		Work effectively with others.
Self Management		Demonstrate self-management by working systematically, persisting with tasks, evaluating and improving own performance.

Personal journal

Some activities are designed to encourage you to keep a personal journal. This will help you understand three key questions:

1 Where have I been?
2 Where am I now?
3 Where do I want to go?

Personal journals will help you make sense of your journey and are a particularly useful tool to help assessment. This means your personal journal may be seen by your teacher, family or classmates. It may be personal but it won't be private!

1 | WHAT ARE THE PARTS THAT MAKE UP A WHOLE PERSON?

Not too many people think of themselves as made up of segments, rather like an orange.

We all know that we are made up of cells and organs and bones and that we need to take care of our bodies or we can get injured or sick. But have you ever thought about what else goes into making you a whole person?

In this topic we will explore all the parts that make us complete human beings, able to live happy and fulfilling lives if we look after and develop our whole selves. The diagram below identifies the parts of a person. These parts work together to make a whole functioning human being.

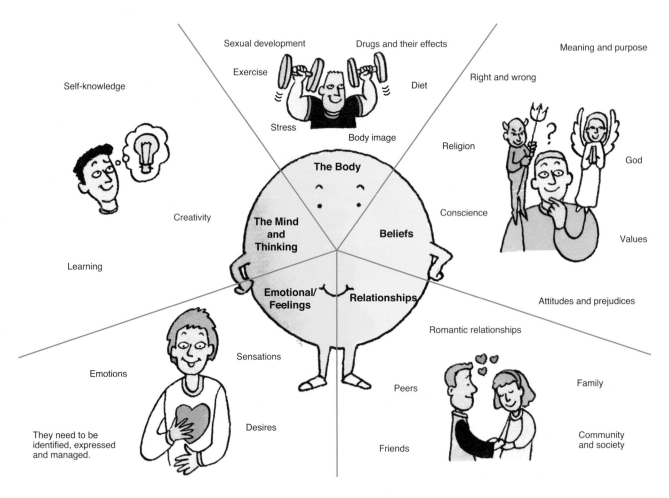

 Activity 1 'I won't be ignored!'

a) What would happen to you if you tried to ignore your need for food? How would this show itself in your body?
b) What would happen if you tried to ignore your conscience or behaved in a way you knew was wrong? How might this show itself in your body?

If we only develop some parts of ourselves and ignore other parts we soon become unbalanced. For example, ignoring our bodies' need for a balanced diet would mean we would feel unhealthy and it would affect our concentration. Ignoring our conscience might mean we become stressed and unable to sleep, which could affect our relationships.

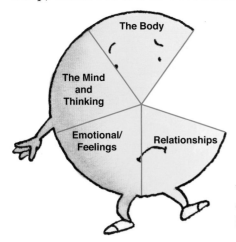

We need to develop each part of ourselves in order to be balanced. What's missing here?

Personal Development is about creating a balance between all the parts that make us whole. If we learn how to look after and develop all our parts, we can become fully balanced and happy. We are able to react to all that life has to offer, deal with the challenges and live life to the full.

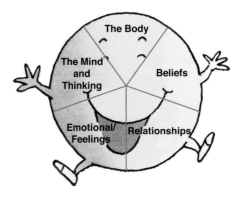

Balance = happiness

 ## Activity 2 What happens if you ignore me?

In groups:

a) Take each part of the person in the diagram opposite and discuss what would happen if you ignored that part and did not spend any time developing it. Record your thoughts on a sheet of paper. For example, 'If I do not look after my body I may suffer from obesity, diabetes or other diseases linked with poor diet.'

b) Now think about what sorts of things you need to do to develop each of these areas. Record a few examples on your sheet. For example, 'Eat a healthy, balanced diet.'

c) Pin your sheets of paper up on the wall. Walk around and see what other groups have said. There should be lots of different thoughts and suggestions, all of them worth considering.

Learning intentions

I am learning:
✓ what being healthy and unhealthy means
✓ different ways of becoming healthy
✓ to take responsibility and set goals to improve my health.

World Health Organisation

An agency of the United Nations, established in 1948 to further international cooperation in improving health conditions.

Activity 2
What do you believe health is?

a) Do you agree with the WHO? In your own words see if you can describe health in a positive way, using all the parts that make you up. Write your own definition and share it with a friend.
'*Health is … (my definition of being healthy).*'

b) If good health is positive and more than not being sick, think through these questions:

■ Can you be a healthy ill person?
■ Can you be an unhealthy well person?

Activity 1 What does being healthy mean?

In pairs:
Discuss the following questions.

■ Would you rather be healthy, happy or rich? Why?
■ How important is health to you?
■ If someone described you as healthy, what would that mean to you?

What is health?

Many of us think 'If I'm not ill or don't feel sick and I don't need a doctor or medical help, I must be healthy!' However, the World Health Organisation (WHO) decided that health is not just physical or a medical problem:

'*Health is much more than not having an illness, a condition or a disease. It is a state of physical, mental and social well-being.*' (WHO, 1948)

This means that health is more than 'not being sick'. It is when all parts of a person are feeling well. It is positive rather than negative.
While health includes our body, it also includes our mind, our feelings, our beliefs, our laws, our finances, our education and the number of choices and opportunities we have.

Activity 3 How healthy are you?

Think of all the parts that make you a whole person (see topic 1).
If each of these parts can be healthy or unhealthy, then how
healthy are you? Decide on a score from 1–5 for each part in the
list below, and then add up the scores. The lower your overall
score, the healthier you think you are.

(1 = healthy, 2 = quite healthy, 3 = in between, 4 = quite unhealthy, 5 = unhealthy.)

a) My relationships   **b)** My body   **c)** My beliefs   **d)** My mind and thinking   **e)** My feelings and emotions

It is unusual to think of taking our
mind to the 'thinking gym' (is that what school is for?),
exercising our feelings, or giving our beliefs a work out!
However, it is important for our personal development to
consider exercising and developing *all* of ourselves.

 # Activity 4 Personal journal

Using the results of activity 3, think of the three key areas where
you need a workout to become healthier. Identify what you need
to do to develop those areas and set some personal targets to
enable you to achieve this.

 # Activity 5 Who's responsible for my health?

a) Who do you think is responsible for you being healthy or
unhealthy? Rank the list below from 1–7 (where 1 = most
responsible, and 7 = least responsible).

- The government (through laws and policies)
- My community   ■ My parents   ■ God
- My school   ■ My doctor   ■ Me

b) Compare your results with the rest of the class. See if you
agree or disagree about who is most responsible for you being
a healthy person.

c) What number have different people in your class put 'Me' at?
Work out the class average, and debate whether you think this
should be changed to be more or less responsible.

Learning intentions

I am learning:
✓ that everyone is unique with their own individual characteristics
✓ to develop helpful strategies to deal with being different from others
✓ to appreciate differences in myself and others.

Everyone in the world is a one-off, unique individual. No one else has ever been, or ever will be the same as you. Everyone has a unique combination of genes, personality, talents and experiences and no one else has the same biology, thoughts, likes and dislikes, mixture of feelings or relationships as you.

You are now entering 'adolescence' (when you are no longer a child, but not yet an adult). It is a time to discover who you are and experiment with what you have to contribute to the world. It's OK not to be sure what you want to be or do and not to have it all worked out just yet.

Activity 1 Being unique

a) In what ways are you similar or different to your family? Think about looks, character, language, jokes and humour, intelligence, interests, etc.

b) Talk to your family tonight and ask them to describe how you have been unique, different and special in your family over the years.

c) Could the world be a better place because you are in it? Why or why not?

d) In 100 years from now, what special thing would you like to be remembered for as your unique contribution to life, history and the human race?

e) In groups:
Share some of your hopes and dreams for the future.

Being comfortable being unique

What is so special about being a one-off? So what? Learning to think carefully about the fact that you are 'different' to anyone else that has ever been is very exciting or difficult to come to terms with. How do you feel about being unique? Does being unique make you special or a freak?

The way we think about our differences is very important and can have a big impact on our lives. If we get into the habit of magnifying how we feel so that our differences become distorted and much bigger or worse than they really are, we certainly don't feel good inside and it affects our relationships and sense of well being.

How do I deal inside with the fact that I am unique and different? We can choose to think helpfully or unhelpfully. For example, if I am the largest person in my class, I might think 'No one could possibly like me because I am so fat' (unhelpful), or 'There is so much more of me to love and appreciate than anyone else' (more helpful).

Activity 2 Coming to terms with being different

Here are four people who are considered to be 'different' in their class.

Sarah

Jim

Li

John

In groups:
Copy the grid below four times (one for each person above). If you were this person, what would you think, feel and do about being different in this way? Think of a way that is positive/helpful and a way that is negative/unhelpful for each situation.

SARAH	Positive/Helpful	Negative/Unhelpful
Thoughts		
Feelings		
Actions		

 ## Activity 3 Class celebration

Form a line around the room. Get each person in turn to go down the line, shaking hands, giving high fives, with lots of cheers and celebrations. Everyone should say something *positive* to the person as they pass them down the line, to show their appreciation of them and to celebrate the fact they bring something unique and special to your class. For example, '*I like your humour*', '*You are a brilliant artist*', '*You make good choices*', '*You are very kind*', or '*You are a loyal friend*', etc.

 ## Activity 4 Personal journal

a) What have you learned from activity 3 about being unique and different?
b) Do you view your differences as positive or negative?
c) Is there anything about yourself you would like to change? If so, why?

4 | CAN I SAY HOW I FEEL?

Learning intentions

I am learning:

✓ to put my feelings into words
✓ that feelings have different strengths and intensities
✓ how to learn from the experiences of others when exploring feelings and emotions.

It is important to be able to recognise and express our feelings in order to show, for example, appreciation, admiration, sadness, anger, fear and disappointment.

In order to do this we need to learn a range of words to put a name to how we feel. The words we choose to use can also help us express the force or strength of that feeling. If we can identify and express the feeling and its intensity, we can then begin to manage our feelings.

Activity 1 Describing feelings

In groups:

a) Collect six large sheets of paper and a marker pen. In the centre of each piece of paper write one of the following words:

■ HAPPINESS ■ SADNESS ■ ANGER ■ PEACE ■ POWER ■ FEAR

b) Take one sheet at a time and in your group think of as many other words that you could use that also describe or link to this feeling. Write them all around the page making a spider diagram – you could also add symbols to your diagram to help describe the words. An example is given opposite.

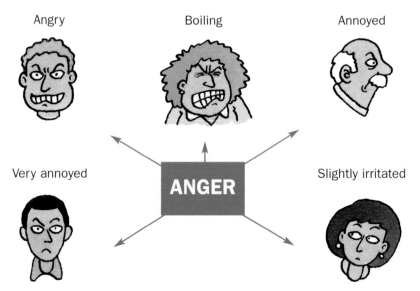

Activity 2 Identifying my feelings

a) Individually:
Read the statements below and, using the sheets of paper from activity 1, pick out words that most closely describe the way you would feel if that situation happened to you.

■ Everyone forgot your birthday.
■ You lent a CD to a friend who now says you didn't.
■ You were caught mitching school.
■ You watched a cat play with a live mouse.
■ A teacher who usually criticises your work, praises you highly.

■ You were told you had won a two-week holiday in London for two with £500 to spend.

b) In groups:
Compare the words you picked with the others in your group and answer the following questions:

■ Did everyone pick the same words for every situation?
■ If not, why not?
■ What does this tell you about people and their feelings?

Personal Development

Activity 3 Intensity of feelings

In groups:

a) Look at all the words on your sheets of paper from activity 1 again. Try to arrange the word by the strength of that feeling, rather like a thermometer – the strongest words would go at the top and the mildest words at the bottom. An example of a thermometer is given opposite.

Copy out six thermometers on separate pages, one for each feeling, and arrange the words in order of strength.

b) Now each member of the group should take one thermometer. Beside each feeling word on the thermometer diagram:

- ■ write an example of a situation that would cause you to have that intensity of feeling
- ■ write an example of how you might express that feeling.

c) Come back together as a group and discuss the situations you have identified for each feeling and how you would express it. Would others have reacted to the situation you have identified in the same way? Why, or why not?

Situations	How do I feel?		What I feel like doing
My mother grounds me for coming in late.	Boiling	100	Feel like hitting, kicking, shouting. Heart pounding.
My sister/brother won't help with the washing up.	Angry		Shoulders hunched, mutter verbal abuse that the other person cannot hear.
A teacher accuses me of something, unjustly.	Very annoyed	50	Tense shoulders, tight mouth, tight stomach. Feel like cursing.
A friend loses my CD and refuses to replace it.	Annoyed		Tight lipped, chest tight, resentful. Feel like complaining loudly.
A friend is late for a film we are all going to see.	Slightly irritated		Slight tensing of body. Foot tapping. Feel impatient and want to snap at them.

Not everyone reacts to situations in the same way. We all express our feelings in different ways and at different levels. A movie may make your mum cry but you may not be sad at all! You may think something is extremely funny but your friend may be only mildly amused or even offended.

It is important to be able to identify and admit to our feelings. They are formed as a result of many things including all the experiences we have had since we were born.

 # Activity 4
Personal journal

Try to identify the feelings you have throughout the course of one day and find words to describe the strength of these feelings.

Learning intentions

I am learning:

✓ the way in which feelings can be shown through body language

✓ how different factors such as age, gender, culture and religion affect how people show their feelings

✓ to understand how actions and words affect me and others.

In topic 4 you learned how different words can be used to describe feelings and their strength. In this topic we are going to explore how, without words, our body language and actions can show what we are feeling inside and also act as a release for our emotions. An example of this is crying when we are sad, which can help us let go of our feelings and feel better afterwards.

So what language does the body use to show feelings?

Activity 1 What language does my body speak?

Individually:

a) Look at the cartoons below and match each one with one of the following captions:

A 'I'm so happy I can't stop smiling!'

B 'I'm red-faced with embarrassment!'

C 'I'm feeling scared – look at my goosebumps!'

D 'I'm so angry, I feel I'm going to explode!'

E 'I'm so sad that I can't stop crying!'

F 'My palms are all sweaty because I'm nervous!'

b) Now record a situation or experience that resulted in you feeling and responding in that way.

c) In groups:

Compare your answers and make a list under each feeling.

Discuss:

■ The range of situations within your group that result in the same emotional response.

■ How the situations you have identified might differ if you were five years younger or five years older.

Personal Development

Activity 2 We are all different

Individually:

a) Think of a word or phrase which would best describe how you would feel in each of the situations on the right. (Refer back to the work you did in topic 4 if you need to.)

b) How would your body show the feeling you would have in each situation?

c) In groups:

Compare your results by discussing the following:

■ Would you all react in the same way in each situation?

■ Would you all react with the same intensity of feeling in each situation?

■ If not, why do you think this is?

■ What conclusions can you come to about how and why people react to different situations in different ways?

How different people express their emotions can depend on what they are like as an individual but also on their age, culture, gender, religion, etc. Let's take age as an example.

As we grow older, the way in which we express how we feel changes. Think of a toddler who has just been told they cannot have another biscuit!

 # Activity 3 Learning to manage feelings

As a class:

a) Discuss how the toddler might demonstrate their feelings.

b) List all the class suggestions on a flipchart under the heading: 'How a toddler behaves'.

c) How would you behave if you asked for a biscuit and were refused one? List all suggestions on the flipchart under the heading: 'How a young person behaves'.

d) Discuss the differences you have identified (hopefully there are some!).

e) Individually:

Answer the following questions:

■ Why do you think a toddler demonstrates their feelings differently to a young person?

■ Why would you not behave the same way as a toddler?

■ What happens to our feelings and how we express them as we grow older?

It's not just age that affects how we express our feelings. Being a boy or girl, the relationship we are in, or our religion or culture will affect the way feelings are expressed.

Situations

1 A younger brother/sister keeps talking during your favourite TV programme.

2 You are standing in line waiting to get an injection.

3 Your favourite t-shirt was shrunk in the wash and now no longer fits.

4 You are walking down an empty side street at night when you hear footsteps behind you.

5 Someone in the playground insults your family name.

6 You are walking home one evening past an old graveyard and you think you see a strange shadow standing over a grave.

6 | CAN I CONTROL HOW I FEEL?

Is it always a good idea to express our feelings in any situation? No! Sometimes it is important to control our feelings in order to make sure we don't harm ourselves and others.

In topic 5 you thought about how a toddler expresses their feelings differently from you. This is because a toddler has not yet begun to learn the important life skill of managing and controlling their feelings. This is the age where they should begin to be taught how to manage their feelings and then, throughout their life, keep learning how to develop the skill. It is not an easy skill to understand and develop, but there are some techniques that can help.

There are many different emotions, and there are many ways to express them. Let's explore what you have been learning about naming and expressing your feelings, to see if we can go on to understand how to manage them more helpfully and healthily.

✓✗ Activity 1 Expressing our emotions

a) Individually:

Read through the situation on the left, then answer the following questions:

■ What thoughts and feelings would you have in this situation?

■ How would you express and let those feelings out?

■ What would be the results of what you say and do in response to those feelings?

b) In groups:

Share your answers and identify the differences and the similarities between you by discussing the following questions:

■ Would you all have the same thoughts and feelings in this situation? Why or why not?

■ Would you all express your feelings the same way?

■ Whose way of expressing emotions had the best results or consequences?

■ Are all the ways we express our feelings as good as each other?

Situation

You are really excited because you and your friend are going to a party tonight to celebrate another friend's birthday. Everybody has been talking about it, and you can't wait. Your friend has arranged with his mum to pick you up at 7:30p.m. and take you both there. At 6:30p.m. your friend phones you and says that he isn't going any more, that he won't be picking you up and that he will see you at school tomorrow – then he hangs up.

Let's use a picture to model a technique that can be used to change our feelings, or how we express them.

Can you picture yourself as a car with four wheels? Each of the four wheels represents different parts of your responses to the situation. They include:

1 Your body responses: the reactions in your body – cold, hot, red face, trembling, sick, calm, restless, sweaty, butterflies in your stomach, etc.
2 Your feelings: the emotion that wells up inside in response to the situation.
3 Your thoughts: what you think about what has happened, its causes and who is responsible.
4 Your actions: what you do in response to your thoughts and feelings.

In most cars you can only steer the front two wheels, and when you do you can move the car in different directions. You can't usually steer the back two wheels directly, but when you steer the front two wheels, the back two will always follow in line.

If you focus on your body responses, or on your feelings, and try to change them, you will almost always fail, because these are involuntary responses that you do not choose. However, if you change the way you think about a situation, as well as changing what you are doing in a situation, your feelings and body responses will follow and change in a different direction (sometimes sooner, sometimes later)! You can change your feelings by changing your thinking about a situation or by changing your behaviour when in a situation.

So let's see if this works by doing activity 2 …

Activity 2
Changing and managing emotions

Individually:
a) Consider again the situation of your friend letting you down about the party. What could you do that would:

- Change your thoughts about what your friend has said and done so that they are more positive?
- Change how you behave after what your friend has said and done to be more positive?

b) How would these changes affect your feelings and body responses for the better?

Activity 3
Personal journal

Think about times in your life when you have been afraid, lonely, jealous, or powerless. What could you have done to change your thoughts and actions that would have affected those feelings?

7 HOW DO I DISCOVER WHO I REALLY AM?

Learning intentions

I am learning:

✓ that people can be measured in different ways
✓ about multiple intelligences
✓ to develop the skill of self-assessment.

When we want to measure the length of an object, we use a ruler. In the world of Personal Development, what can we use to measure a human being and how their whole person is growing?

We have some good measuring tools but only for certain parts of our person. For example:

- at school, exams and tests can measure your knowledge
- at the doctors, different medical tests can measure if we are physically well.

Are these the only things we can measure? There is a range of other ways to measure a person and we are going to explore one of these so we can find out more about who we are. We are going to look at various ways of being smart, called multiple intelligences.

A man called Howard Gardner has developed a system that looks at eight different types of intelligence. Not everyone does well with maths or English, but that doesn't mean they are not smart. If you complete the various surveys, they will help give you a more complete understanding and picture of yourself and the different ways that you are smart.

The eight types of intelligence, or ways of being smart include:

1 Body smart: a person who uses their body well by developing good skills in using tools or objects.

2 Word smart: a person who is good at using and ordering words and their meanings.

3 Number smart: ability to handle numbers, sequences, patterns and order. A logical person.

4 People smart: someone who understands people and relationships.

Personal Development

14

5 Myself smart: someone who is aware of what's going on inside in terms of their body and feelings and can use this to understand themselves and others.

6 Music smart: people who are sensitive to rhythm, tone, pitch and melody.

7 Picture smart: someone who sees and learns through pictures and is good at understanding space and creating or transforming things.

8 Nature smart: a person who likes nature and working with natural materials.

Activity 1 How am I smart?

a) In order to find out the ways in which you are smart, you need to complete a survey and then analyse the results. There are two ways you can do this:

1 If you have a computer with internet access:
Look up this site on the internet, which is suitable for young people.
www2.bgfl.org/bgfl2/custom/resources_ftp/client_ftp/ks3/ict/multiple_int/questions/questions.cfm
Or alternatively there is a variety of tests which can be found if you type in 'Multiple intelligence tests' into a search engine.

2 If you don't have access to a computer:
Your teacher will need to download a multiple intelligence test for you. You will then need to add up your scores and work out what they mean for you. An example of a test suitable for young people that could be used is at www.businessballs.com

b) After you have completed and analysed a test complete the following sentence:

'From these tests, my main strengths in terms of multiple intelligences are ...'

Activity 2
Personal journal

Complete the following sentences:

- Today I have learned that I am ...
- My major strengths are ...
- This makes me think ...
- This makes me feel ...
- As a result I want to ...

Learning intentions

I am learning:

✓ what learning is all about
✓ why learning from experience is an essential skill
✓ to see opportunities in the mistakes I make.

Learning is something we do all the time, we just can't help it! It happens even before we are born, when we learn to recognise sound, to swallow and even suck our thumb.

Many things that we learn are essential life skills, like walking and not touching something hot. Other things we learn are about gaining knowledge, like reading instructions for making a model or finding out what caused rusting on a metal gate.

In this topic we will look at how people learn from experience and mistakes, while in topic 9 we will explore some different styles of learning.

 ## Activity 1 What have I learned so far?

In pairs:

a) List all of the key things you have learned to do since you were born.

b) Divide these into knowledge and skills.

c) Now decide whether you learned each thing by being taught, or from experience of trial and error.

d) Record your results in a table like the one below.

Knowledge I have learned	Skills I have learned	Taught	By experience

Often we learn without even realising it. Learning from experience can be one of our most important skills. It teaches us about danger and how to keep safe. It teaches us how to get attention and how to make people laugh. Our learning experiences can be positive like making someone laugh, feeling good because you helped someone, or winning a race. Or they can be negative like cutting your hand on broken glass, feeling guilty because you hurt your friend's feelings, or being scared by a stranger.

 ## Activity 2 Making mistakes

In pairs:

Think about mistakes you have made in the past.

- What types of feelings do you have when you make a mistake?
- Do you have the same feelings for every mistake you make?
- What affects the strength and type of feelings that you have?
- What do you do after making a mistake?

Learning from mistakes

Mistakes are something everyone experiences. In fact, without making mistakes we would find it very hard to learn, or personally develop. This is what learning from experience is all about! School is a safe environment that allows you to make mistakes and learn so that when faced with similar situations in life, you have a range of experiences and skills to help you deal with them.

Skills learned in school are useful in adult life. How does this cartoon show that learning from mistakes can benefit us?

 ## Activity 3 Learning from experience

Below are some quotes by famous people about learning from experience.

a) Explain what each quote means in your own words.

b) Which do you agree or disagree with? Give reasons.

c) Write your own quote to explain how learning from experience can be useful in life.

> 'A failure is a man who has blundered but is not able to cash in on the experience.'
> Elbert Hubbard, American writer, 1856–1915

> 'Human beings are like tea bags. You don't know your own strength until you get into hot water.'
> Bruce Laingen, former American hostage in Iran

> 'Nothing is a waste of time if you use the experience wisely.'
> Auguste Rodin, French sculptor, 1840–1917

> 'Experience is the name everyone gives to their mistakes.'
> Oscar Wilde, Irish novelist/poet 1854–1900

 ## Activity 4 Personal journal

Individually:
Reflect on some experience or mistake you have had or made.

■ What have you learned from this experience?

■ How might it help you in the future?

■ Have you ever kept on making the same mistake? If so, why?

■ Do you think people always learn from their mistakes?

■ What are the possible results for a society that does not learn from experience?

Learning intentions

I am learning:
- ✓ to understand there are different types of learning
- ✓ to explore how I learn best
- ✓ to identify how I could improve my learning.

 Activity 1 Does everyone learn in the same way?

a) Imagine you have just got a new games console and you want to set it up. Do you:
1 Read the written instructions first before doing anything?
2 Look at the diagrams and try to work out what to do?
3 Ask a friend to tell you how to set it up?
4 Ask a friend to show you what to do?
5 Just have a go and figure it out as you go along?

b) Carry out a survey amongst your class to see how many people chose each of the options. Record your results by creating a graph or chart.

The way in which you go about setting up a piece of equipment says a lot about your preferred learning style. It should be clear from your survey results that we do not all prefer to learn to do things in the same way. You could also survey your class to see how they go about revising for a test. Again, you would find that different people use different approaches.

There are many different models to explain learning styles. The one used in this book is called the VAK model.

V = Visual learners learn through seeing ...

Visual learners need to see the teacher's body language and facial expression to fully understand a lesson. They tend to prefer sitting at the front of the classroom to avoid people's heads. They may think in pictures and learn best from visual displays including: diagrams, illustrated textbooks, overhead transparencies, PowerPoint presentations, videos/DVDs, flipcharts and handouts.

A = Auditory learners learn through listening ...

Auditory learners learn best through discussions, talking things through and listening to what others have to say.

 They pick up the meaning of speech through listening to tone of voice, pitch and speed.

Written information may have little meaning until it is heard. These learners often benefit from reading text aloud and using recordings.

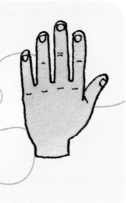

K = Kinaesthetic learners learn through moving, doing and touching ...

Kinaesthetic learners learn best through a hands-on approach, actively exploring the physical world around them. They may find it hard to sit still for long periods and may become distracted by their need for activity and exploration.

 Activity 2 So which learning style are you?

a) You may already have some idea based on your survey results from activity 1 and the descriptions above, but you can find out more accurately by completing a questionnaire. These are available on the internet. Two examples are:
www.brainboxx.co.uk/A3_ASPECTS/pages/VAK.htm **or**
www.businessballs.com/vaklearningstylestest.htm

b) When you have finished the questionnaire calculate your learning style and find out what this means for you.

You will notice that you are a mixture of all three learning styles, but will tend to have a preference for one style. This does not mean that you cannot learn in other ways, just that you will find it easier to learn using some methods more than others. Now that you know what your preferred style is, you can start to change the way you go about tasks to improve your learning.

 Activity 3 Learning styles in practice

a) Choose any task you have to do in school. Think about how you can do it in a way that will suit your preferred learning style.

b) In groups made up of people with the same preferred learning styles, come up with a list of suggestions that will help you all complete your tasks successfully.

c) Try out some of these methods and report back to the group on how successful you thought they were. Different ones may suit different people so you may have to try a few to find the one that's best for you!

 **Activity 4**
Personal journal

a) How does it feel to learn in a way that you find easier?

b) How does it feel to learn in a way that you find difficult?

c) If you can change how you learn so that it is easier, what difference will this make in school?

d) Think of a subject you find difficult. What could you do to make the learning easier?

e) How does enjoying learning make you feel inside?

Learning intentions

I am learning:

✓ about two broad types of relationships
✓ to understand what the point of my relationships are
✓ to identify some important ingredients that make up healthy relationships.

As human beings we are involved in a variety of relationships. Life is all about connecting and engaging with others. Relationships come and go, change and develop and go up and down throughout our lives. In this topic we want to discover what the point is of having relationships.

 Activity 1 Do we need relationships?

In groups discuss:

■ What is the point of having relationships? Why do we need them?
■ What is the point of being in a family?
■ What is the point of belonging to a community?

Discovering more about relationships

For a relationship to exist, two people or groups of people must give and receive something from the relationship. They share their lives in a way that benefits one another. What they give may not be equal, but it should be agreed.

While there are many types of relationship, their purpose can be broadly put into two types:

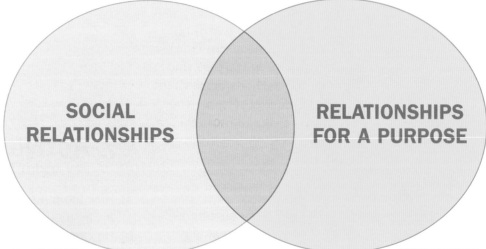

SOCIAL RELATIONSHIPS

RELATIONSHIPS FOR A PURPOSE

Social relationships exist as an end in themselves, and not as a means to an end. The relationship is the purpose! We enter them so we can connect and bond with someone else. Examples are family, friendship or marriage.

Relationships for a purpose are entered into with others in order to achieve something. For example, a dentist and a patient enter a relationship for the benefit of the patient's teeth and dental health.

Most relationships we enter are a mixture of the two types, but one of them will usually be more important. The question is whether we agree which is more important!

 ## Activity 2 Which relationship is which?

In groups:

a) Decide which of the relationships below are mostly social and which are mainly for a purpose.

- Teacher/pupil
- Parent/child
- Boss/worker
- Two pupils in the same class
- Boyfriend/girlfriend
- Clergy and church member

b) Then draw a Venn diagram like the one opposite and place them where you think they should go – are any in the middle?

c) For those relationships which are mainly for a purpose, identify what the purpose is.

 ## Activity 3 What makes a good relationship?

In groups:

a) Think of 'social relationships' and 'relationships for a purpose' as recipes. What ingredients would go into the relationships to make them worth having? Think of five key ingredients for each and place them in order of importance. For example, do love, looks, respect, trust, ability, personality or communication fit in both types or only in one?

b) Compare and contrast what the similarities and differences are between the two types of relationships.

 ## Activity 4 Personal journal

a) Make a list of the people in your life with whom you have a social relationship.

b) Which of your five key ingredients of a social relationship from activity 3 do you display in your relationships? What can you do to enhance these?

c) What three things could you do to help maintain your social relationships so they continue to be healthy?

d) Do you think you have a good mixture of relationships that are both social and for a purpose? Which are most important for you?

WHY IS COMMUNICATION IMPORTANT?

Learning intentions

I am learning:

✓ the part that understanding plays in effective communication

✓ the skill of understanding others

✓ to become more effective in communicating at different levels.

There are three key elements of communication:

1 talking; **2** listening; and **3** understanding.

Many of the serious problems in life happen because of poor communication – like wars, fighting, community or religious conflict, family breakdown and feeling alone. This topic looks at understanding, and how we can develop the skill of understanding others.

 Activity 1 Can I understand you?

In pairs:

- Sit back to back.
- Take turns to sketch a simple object without your partner seeing the drawing.
- Now communicate to your partner how to draw the object you have sketched so that the two drawings are as similar as possible (same size, shape, shading, etc.).
- You have two minutes to do this!
- Compare the two drawings after two minutes to see what you 'understood' from what was said.
- The rules to this activity are simple – you can't look at all, you can't name the object (e.g. you can't say it's a heart or an apple), and you must sit back to back, using only words (not hand signals) to convey an understanding of what has to be drawn.

 Activity 2 Thinking about understanding

In groups:

Discuss the questions below based on your experience of activity 1:

- What does it feel like when you are understood?
- What does it feel like when you are not understood?
- What needs to happen between two people in order to understand what is being communicated? (Use the diagram opposite to help your discussion.)
- How much work is it to understand people?

Communicator

My Message

The **Communication Process**

Receiver

The Message that is actually understood

My Message working through my...
- Culture
- Body language
- Education
- Motives
- Attitudes
- Environment
- Experiences
- Etc.

The Message working through my...
- Culture
- Body language
- Education
- Motives
- Attitudes
- Environment
- Experiences
- Etc.

The **Expression** of my Message

The **Impression** of my Message

Personal Development

Levels of communication

Communication is not what we say, but what people understand from what we say!

Here are five levels at which we can communicate. Each level can allow us to be better understood, but it is also more scary because people can reject the real us! Understanding is hard work and involves different levels of risk.

Clichés: When we use common phrases that are polite but say very little, e.g. 'Lovely day, how are you?' 'Fine, thank you. Have a nice day!'

Facts: When we share factual information, without giving away our opinions or feelings, e.g. 'Did you know that a Year 8 in our school won the art competition?'

Opinions: We share with others what we think about things, e.g. 'Paul won the art competition and I think it is about time our school was recognised!'

Feelings: We share with others what we feel about things, e.g. 'I am glad that Paul won, but sad that I didn't.'

Openness and honesty: When we share what we think without any attempt to look better, be politically correct or pretend, e.g. 'I feel jealous and threatened by Paul's artistic ability.'

Levels of communication

 **Activity 3** Communicating at different levels

In pairs:
- **a)** Agree a topic to talk about with your partner, e.g. football, religion or school dinners, etc.
- **b)** Talk about your chosen subject with each other for five minutes at the different levels of communication above:
  - first minute only meaningless clichés
  - second minute only facts
  - third minute opinions
  - fourth minute feelings
  - last minute as open and honest as you dare.
- **c)** Once finished, reflect back to each other how difficult, easy or helpful you found each level. Do you feel you understand each other better now or not?

 **Activity 4**
Personal journal

Score yourself on statements a)–c) below and then reflect on your ability to understand others and to be understood.
(1 = strongly agree, 2 = agree, 3 = not sure, 4 = disagree, 5 = strongly disagree.)

- **a)** I work hard to understand others when they communicate with me.
- **b)** I feel that nobody understands me.
- **c)** I can communicate at a deep level with someone in my life.

Learning intentions

I am learning:
- ✓ what boundaries are
- ✓ why boundaries are important
- ✓ to set up boundaries in my life.

Activity 1 What do I want in my life?

Go through the list of words below. Get two different coloured pens or pencils, e.g. black and red, and make two lists.

- List 1 should include all the things that you want in your life, in black. (Add any you want that aren't listed.)
- List 2 should include all the things that you don't want in your life in red. (Add any you don't want that aren't listed.)
- Identify the top three things you do want and the top three things you don't want, in order of priority.

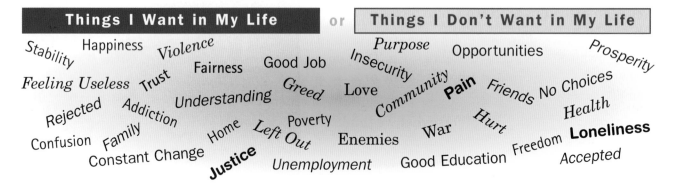

Things I Want in My Life or **Things I Don't Want in My Life**

Stability Happiness Violence Purpose Opportunities Prosperity
Feeling Useless Trust Fairness Good Job Insecurity Pain Friends No Choices
Rejected Addiction Understanding Greed Love Community Hurt Health
Confusion Family Constant Change Home Left Out Poverty Enemies War Freedom Loneliness
Justice Unemployment Good Education Accepted

All of us want lives that are worth living. We try to keep good things in and keep bad things out. In order to do this, we create boundaries around our lives to protect us.

What are boundaries?

Boundaries are lines, borders or things that define limits, e.g.:

- walls like the Great Wall of China (protecting a nation)
- fences around a house (defining your property)
- rules in a school (limits around behaviour)
- a prison cell (limiting choices and freedom)
- your face (defining you).

There are three main purposes to having boundaries:

1 Safety, protection and security: boundaries help create a safe or safer place that contain us and protect us from harm.
2 Freedom within limits: once we create a safe place, we are more free to enjoy ourselves and are free to be ourselves without hiding or being afraid.
3 To define something and create identity: boundaries help us realise we are a person in our own right, apart from others. This sense of being separate forms the basis of identity and of being special or unique. They help us know who we are and what we will do/not do.

The Great Wall of China

What are personal boundaries?

Personal boundaries are like a door over your life. They are boundaries that you set yourself. Some things you want to allow in, others you want to keep out at all costs. You need to train hard and develop muscle and a strong will to be a good bouncer who can open or close the door to ensure your boundaries are effective. The diagram shows some boundaries you may want to let in and out and others which you would want to keep out.

Personal boundaries are both the limits you put around your life and also the limits others put around you, such as laws, rules, etc. to get both maximum happiness *and* safety. So what boundaries will help you create a safe freedom but avoid making a prison?

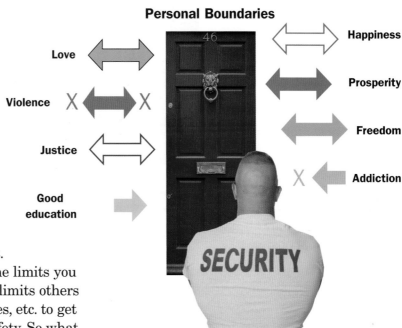

Personal Boundaries

Love

Violence

Justice

Good education

Happiness

Prosperity

Freedom

Addiction

SECURITY

 ## Activity 2 Our personal boundaries

In groups:
Copy out the table opposite. Come up with a personal boundary for each of the five topics suggested (add as many as you wish). The boundary can be positive, e.g. 'I will always eat green vegetables', or negative, e.g. 'It's not OK for others to spread rumours about me'.

Personal area	Our personal boundary
Telling lies to my parents	
Diet and nutrition	
What feelings I will express/ not express	
Saving money	
Gossiping	

 ## Activity 3 To have or not to have boundaries?

In pairs:
- Discuss what might happen to a person when they have too rigid a boundary. For example, 'I will never trust anyone in my life again!' or 'I will not believe anything my teacher says.'
- Discuss what might happen to a person when they have no boundaries. For example, 'Anyone can say or do anything to me that they want to and I won't object', or 'I can take any drug I like.'
- How important is it to set personal boundaries in your life?

 ## Activity 4 Personal journal

Think of the three most important boundaries for you to set up and maintain in your life. These should help you keep good things in and protect you by keeping unhealthy things out.

Learning intentions

I am learning:

✓ to reflect on my own attitudes towards change by exploring my feelings when changes happen

✓ to work with a partner to explore how attitudes towards change can affect someone's behaviour

✓ to ask myself focused questions to find out how I think and react in different situations.

From the moment of conception, a human being starts a process of change that will continue for the rest of their life. Cells are dividing and growing. The brain is developing and learning to react and respond to all sorts of things ...

... Our environment is constantly changing too. New buildings and roads, changing weather, new technology, new governments and even new countries change the way the world is shaped.

When you think about it, nothing ever stays the same, it isn't supposed to.

However, some changes can be unexpected, unplanned and even threatening. They may cause sadness and hurt and can be very hard to manage – for example, changing school, moving to a new area, emigrating to a new country, or the death of a family member.

 ## Activity 1 Changes in my life

Individually:

a) Record as many changes that you can remember that made a significant difference in your life.

b) Decide if the impact was small, medium or large. Examples of an impact might be on your time, freedom, money, friendships, confidence, personal responsibility, etc.

c) Describe how the change made you feel, e.g. sad, nervous, anxious, excited, lonely, proud, happy, secure, etc.

d) Did you think about the change as a good or bad thing?

e) Record your answers in a table like the one below.

Description of the change that took place	Level and type of impact (Small, Medium, Large)	How the change made me feel	Good or bad
Moving to secondary school.	Medium impact on my confidence and friendships.	Nervous about getting lost and a bit sad because my best friend had gone to a different school.	Good – because moving on to a new stage in my life.

For some people, change is an unpleasant thing which upsets their everyday routine and they view it as negative. For example, at secondary school you probably have to move from room to room and carry all your books, rather than staying in one classroom like in primary school.

However, many changes can bring us new experiences and help us grow and develop by creating the potential for us to develop new skills and strategies to manage the change. For example, in secondary school you get the opportunity to do new subjects and learn new skills when doing practical subjects like technology.

Looked at this way, change can provide us with new opportunities and keep us motivated and fresh.

When you changed from primary to secondary school, your thoughts about changing school will have influenced your attitude and how you felt. This in turn will have affected how you behaved.

How is your secondary school different from your primary school?

 ## Activity 2 Does the way we think affect how we behave?

In pairs:
a) Draw a table like the one below.
b) Discuss and list what you think the thoughts and actions of someone with a positive attitude towards changing schools would be (an example has been given).
c) Discuss and list what you think the thoughts and actions of someone with a negative attitude towards changing schools would be (an example has been given).

	Positive thinker	Negative thinker
Thoughts	There will be lots of new subjects I haven't done before and we will get to use computers and do science experiments.	I won't know anybody and the bigger pupils will bully me. I will get lost and the teachers will shout at me.
Actions	Gets up in the morning without any persuasion and is enthusiastic during class discussions, taking an active part in all activities.	Slow to get up in the morning. Complains about feeling sick and not wanting to go to school. Doesn't join in the class discussions or get involved in school activities.

d) Discuss which way of thinking is going to be the most beneficial and use your table to provide evidence to back up your answer.

 ## Activity 3
Personal journal

a) What about you? Do you see change as an opportunity or a threat?
b) Can you give examples of when you felt both?
c) Which one had the best outcome?

Learning intentions

I am learning:
- ✓ to define what values are
- ✓ which values are most important to me
- ✓ how I arrived at my values.

In order to make the most of life, we try to organise it in the most helpful way. To help us, we value some ideas and activities more than others. These values are what shape our beliefs and they guide how we behave. The engine of a car, though not seen when the car is moving, is the key thing that moves it – our values, though not seen, help drive what we do. In order to understand ourselves and how we behave, we need to know what our values are.

 ## Activity 1 Defining values

In pairs:

Try to come up with a definition of what a 'value' is, in words that make sense to you. Try to work it out yourselves first, then, if necessary, consult a dictionary, thesaurus or the internet.

 ## Activity 2 Which values are important to you?

Rank in order the following values, from the most important to the least important to you (1 = most important, 14 = least important).

A. Honesty

B. Lots of money

C. An exciting life

D. A world of peace

E. Health

F. Clear beliefs that shape your life

G. Self-respect

H. Loyal friendship

I. Intelligence

J. Family togetherness

K. Equality (equal rights for everyone)

L. A healthy environment

M. Freedom

N. Another value important to me.

If we value something, we believe it to be important, or we have a high opinion of it. We can value things like gold or diamonds, or people whom we believe to be priceless. We can value behaviour, like being honest or not telling lies. Or we can value ideas or beliefs – like a religion, politics, science or the law.

A value is what we judge to be important in life, and from these we develop principles and standards that guide what we do or don't do. They determine what we like or don't like. They establish what we think is right or wrong, helpful or unhelpful, acceptable or unacceptable.

 ## Activity 3 Exploring where my values come from

a) Based on your answer to activity 2, complete the following sentences.

■ My three most important values are:

  1._____

  2._____

  3._____

■ My least important value is: _____

b) Take your three most important values from part a), and using the diagram below, work out where these values came from in your life.

c) Can you think of any other influences not shown in the diagram?

d) Are any of your values just your own and not influenced by anything around you?

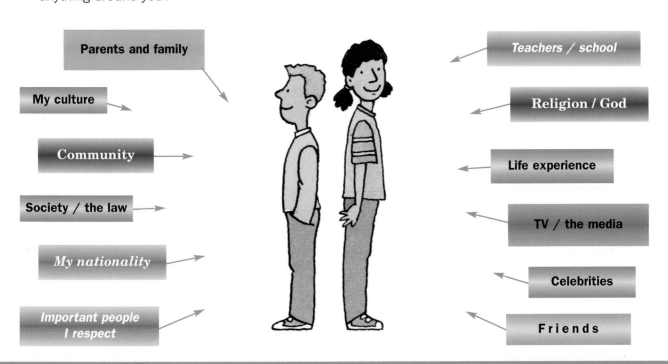

Learning intentions

I am learning:

✓ what influences have an impact on the decisions I make

✓ how to make informed decisions by examining options and weighing up pros and cons.

Imagine the situation

You need a new coat for the winter. Your friend has just got a new one and you think it looks really good and you've seen a similar one advertised on TV, but it is really expensive! Your mum is taking you shopping to buy a coat and when you try the one you like on, it's not very warm and your mum is concerned about the price. There are other cheaper coats in the shop and more practical too! She says that it's up to you to make the decision as you will be wearing the coat.

So, what will influence your decision? Friends, TV, price, practicality (warmth), or parent?

Everyone has to make decisions every day. Some are easy, 'What will I have for breakfast?' some are a lot more difficult, 'What school do I want to go to?' or 'Will I take a puff of that cigarette?'

 Activity 1 Who influences my decisions?

Individually:

a) Copy and complete the table below to consider the sorts of decisions you have to make and who influences you. Add more influences if you wish.

Some decisions might have more than one influence – if so rank them in order of importance, with '1' being the most important.

Who influences ...	Parents	Friends	Teachers	TV/Media	Celebrities	Other
What you wear?						
What you do after school?						
Who you meet in the evenings?						
How hard you work in school?						
What time you go to bed?						
Whether to drink alcohol or not?						
Which magazines you read?						
Which DVDs to watch?						
What you eat?						

b) Use the data from the table to help you decide who is the biggest influence in your life.

■ Give an example of the way in which this person/s has a positive influence on you, e.g. encourages you to keep fit by going swimming after school.

■ If you can, give an example of the way in which this person/s has a negative influence on you, e.g. encourages you to tell lies about why you were late home after school.

■ How can you make sure that the influence this person/s has on you is positive rather than negative?

Personal Development

How many times have you made a decision which you have regretted later? It happens to us all! We say to ourselves, 'I didn't think that would happen!' or 'If only I had thought about that first, I would never have made that decision!'

There is a way to make better decisions, but it takes a bit of practice and self-discipline. The next activity should give you some tools to help you in your decision-making skills.

An informed decision is when you make that decision based on evidence you have gathered together. Below is a framework to help you make an informed decision.

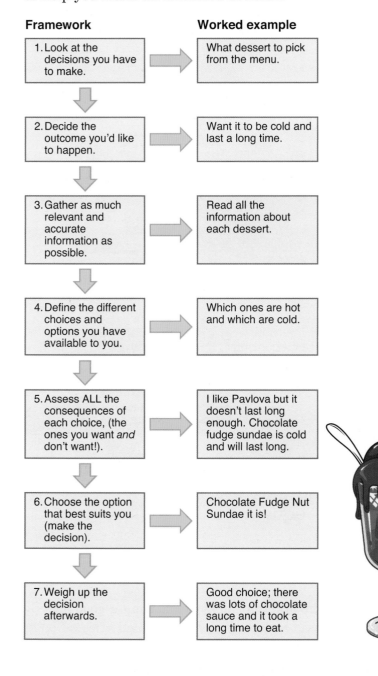

Framework

1. Look at the decisions you have to make.
2. Decide the outcome you'd like to happen.
3. Gather as much relevant and accurate information as possible.
4. Define the different choices and options you have available to you.
5. Assess ALL the consequences of each choice, (the ones you want *and* don't want!).
6. Choose the option that best suits you (make the decision).
7. Weigh up the decision afterwards.

Worked example

What dessert to pick from the menu.

Want it to be cold and last a long time.

Read all the information about each dessert.

Which ones are hot and which are cold.

I like Pavlova but it doesn't last long enough. Chocolate fudge sundae is cold and will last long.

Chocolate Fudge Nut Sundae it is!

Good choice; there was lots of chocolate sauce and it took a long time to eat.

Activity 2
Making an informed decision

Use your ICT skills to organise the seven steps in the framework into a table or flowchart with space to fill in the information you will require to successfully make a decision. Use the decision below, or use some of your own to put the framework into practice.

Decision

You arrive at PE to discover your teacher is off sick. The cover teacher offers the class a choice but it has to be a majority decision. Which would you choose?
a) Basketball
b) Gymnastics or
c) a free study period.

Activity 3
Personal journal

Think of a decision you made recently that you would like to have changed.

■ Why would you want to change it?
■ What would you like to have done instead?
■ Do you think using the framework will help you make better decisions in the future?

Learning intentions

I am learning:

✓ to recognise a range of views about what 'citizenship' means

✓ to identify the knowledge and skills that are needed to become a more effective citizen.

Local and Global Citizenship is about discovering how you can get involved in the issues that affect the communities you belong to, for example your school, your local area, your town, your country and the wider world. To do this you need to develop your knowledge about key issues affecting society so you can make better choices. You will also need to develop skills to help you play an effective and active part in today's world. During the course of the next few years you will be exploring a range of topics, concepts and ideas. These make up the pieces of the Local and Global Citizenship jigsaw! By the end of the course you should be able to connect all of these ideas into one big picture. Here is a taster of what is in store.

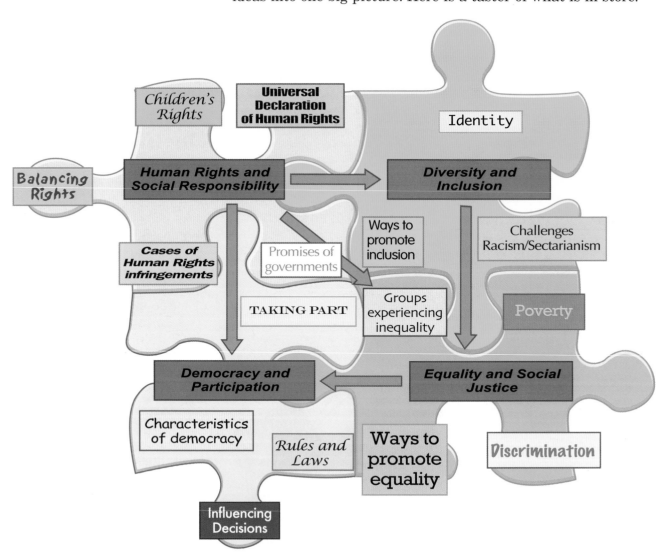

Different people have different ideas about what a good or effective citizen should be like. Carry out the activities on page 33 to help you explore what *you* think.

Activity 1 A good citizen?

In groups:

a) Copy the thermometer on the right onto a large piece of paper.

b) Decide whether you *agree* with, *disagree* with or *feel unsure* about the statements A–I below.

c) Discuss these with your group and place them onto the part of the thermometer that you feel fits best.

d) Share your conclusions with the rest of the class and justify the decisions your group made.

A A good citizen supports the police.
B A good citizen has a job.
C A good citizen always respects the government.
D A good citizen obeys the law.
E A good citizen will speak out against injustice.
F A good citizen keeps to themselves.
G A good citizen involves themselves in what's going on in the world.
H A good citizen never wants to offend anyone.
I A good citizen has strong religious convictions.

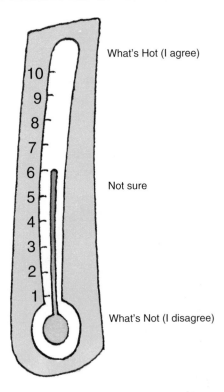

 # Activity 2 The effective citizen

Individually:

a) Draw a silhouette of a person on a page.

b) Label it like the example provided on the right with what you think are the characteristics of an effective citizen. For example, the person's brain might help you think about what knowledge an effective citizen might need, the heart might deal with the things they need to care about, while the hands, mouth, head, feet, etc. might be useful to get you thinking about what skills are needed.

In groups:

c) Compare your answers and agree a list of the main things needed to be an effective citizen.

d) Record these key features under the headings: 'knowledge' and 'skills' in your journal.

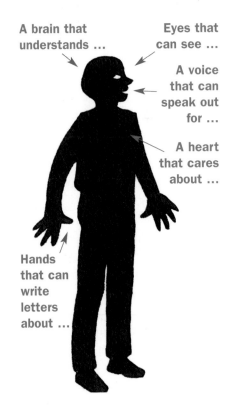

 # Activity 3 Personal journal

In your journal draw a silhouette of yourself in the centre of a page and answer the following questions. Record your answers around the outside of the picture.

- What knowledge will I need to make me a more effective citizen?
- What issues do I need to study that might make me a more effective citizen?
- What skills do I need to develop that might help me become a more effective citizen?

Learning intentions

I am learning:

✓ to prioritise what is needed to help people develop fully as human beings

✓ to explain the term 'human rights'.

Bono, lead singer of the band, U2

In topic 16 you learned that Local and Global Citizenship is based on four themes. The next six topics will help you to begin exploring the theme of human rights and social responsibility.

Amnesty International has said that, '*Human beings have human rights whatever label they are given and wherever they are.*' They are not the only people who talk about human rights.

Take the pop singer Bono, for example. Using U2's worldwide fame he is able to draw attention to many human rights issues. Over the last two decades, Bono has visited the starving in Ethiopia, spoken out about the need for peace in Northern Ireland and has campaigned for debt relief. In April 2005 at a concert in San Diego he said that he wanted human rights to be a reality in everyone's lives.

But when we hear people talking about human rights, we need to ask ourselves: what do we really mean by human rights?

Look at the diagram below. Catherine has just been born into the world. Her life has just begun. She is totally dependent on the people around her to look after her but she will grow up to be a young person just like you and some day an adult. But what will she need to help her grow up and develop?

Activity 1
What do I need?

Individually:

a) Copy the spider diagram but use a photograph of yourself as a baby, or write Catherine's name in the centre. Write down *your* answers to the questions around the outside in a different colour.

As a group:

b) Compare your answers and agree a list of the top ten things the baby will *need* as she goes through her life.

c) Record this list of 'Top Ten Needs'.

What will Catherine need to *survive* and be safe?

What will Catherine need to *learn* about the world around her?

What will Catherine need to help her *develop* her talents?

What will Catherine need to help her *make decisions* as she grows up?

What will Catherine need to give her the *same chances* as everyone else, as she grows up?

We all need basic things to help us survive like food and shelter. But there is more to being human than just *surviving*. We need to be able to *develop* and learn about the world around us. We also need to be *protected* from harm and given a chance to have a say or participate in our society. So if we *need* all these things then surely it is only right that we *have* them. All of these basic needs that we should have are what we mean when we talk about human rights.

 ## Activity 2 Sort out your rights!

a) In your groups:

- Look at your Top Ten Needs list from activity 1.
- Circle anything in the list that you need to **survive**.
- Underline anything in the list that you need to **develop**.
- Highlight anything in the list that you need for **protection**.
- Put a box around anything in the list that you need for **participation**.

b) Individually:
Write down examples of human rights under the four headings in part a) above.

 ## Activity 3 Personal journal

Human rights experts have defined human rights in a number of different ways. Look at the four definitions on this page.

Choose one of the four definitions that you think best explains what we mean by human rights, or write your own definition and record this in your journal. Explain why you have chosen this definition.

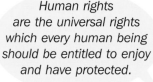

In the last topic *you* decided on a set of basic needs or human rights that everyone in the world should be entitled to. In this topic you will learn about why it is important to protect the human rights of everyone around the world.

Imagine that you have been asked to prepare a speech about why it is important to protect human rights. Speeches need to be persuasive and informative. The information below will help you to gather some facts and ideas – so read it carefully. The activities will help you to structure your speech.

Activity 1
Why protect human rights?

a) Complete and answer the following, this can be the first part of your speech:

All around the world people are denied their basic h_____ r_____. In _____ women were not allowed to _____.

b) Why were so many people killed in Cambodia?

c) What do *you* think were wrong with the Nazi laws described opposite?

d) Why do *you* think there is a need to protect human rights?

◀ The Taliban were religious leaders who ruled Afghanistan from 1996 to 2001. Under their rule women couldn't go out in public unless they had a close male relative with them. Women were banned from most types of employment and girls could only receive a primary school education. Ninety per cent of woman in Afghanistan couldn't read or write.

▶ In 1930s Nazi Germany, Jews were barred from various jobs. They had to register their property so that the state could take it from them by paying them a fraction of what it was truly worth. Jews had to wear the Star of David to identify them. These measures helped to separate them from the rest of German society so that they could be treated differently and cruelly.

◀ Pol Pot was a dictator in the 1970s in Cambodia. He ordered the execution of around one million people whose views and lifestyles he disagreed with. He did this because he wanted to get rid of all aspects of Western culture from Cambodia. His army, the Khmer Rouge, were used to torture and execute thousands of innocent people, including the people in this photo.

The Universal Declaration Of Human Rights

After the terrible things that happened in the Second World War, many countries came together and formed the United Nations. Their main task was to write a document that would be used to protect human rights.

They called the document the Universal Declaration of Human Rights (UDHR). It was signed on 10 December 1948 by all the countries that made up the United Nations at that time. By signing it these countries promised to promote and protect the human rights listed in this document.

The human rights contained in the UDHR are sometimes called 'entitlements' because they are things that we should all have simply because we are human beings, e.g. the right to life, shelter, protection, etc. There are 30 statements in the UDHR. Each statement is called an 'article'. Sometimes a country may break some of these articles. When this happens, it is said to be a violation of an article of the UDHR.

This picture shows children learning about the UDHR after it was signed.

 ## Activity 2 The Universal Declaration

a) Complete and answer the following, this can be the second part of your speech:

On 10 D_____ in the year _____ many countries came together to form the U_____ N_____ and to make a list of h_____ r_____ for everyone in the world. They called this list the U_____ D_____ of H_____ R_____.

b) Why did the United Nations do this?   **c)** Why do *you* think the UDHR is so important?

 ## Activity 3 The final speech

a) Now that you have completed a basic speech, you may want to gather extra information to make your speech more informative and persuasive. Here are some ideas:

- Could any of your other school subjects give you more *information* of cases where human rights have been violated (e.g. History, RE)?
- Could any of the skills you have developed in other subjects help you to make your speech more *persuasive* (e.g. English)?
- Could you search the internet for more information?

b) Use all the information you have gathered to write your speech.

c) As a class decide on at least five things or 'criteria' that make a speech informative and persuasive, e.g. thorough research, a clear speaking voice, the use of ICT or pictures, etc. Record this list in your journal.

d) Present your speech to other members of your class.

 ## Activity 4
Personal journal

Use the 'criteria' generated by your class to reflect on how well your *own* speech was produced and presented. Record this in your journal and assess your own performance by giving yourself a comment or a mark for each of the 'criteria'. Finally record what you would do to *improve* on your performance if you were asked to give a speech again.

Learning intentions

I am learning:

✓ to work with others and to communicate ideas to the rest of the class

✓ about the types of promises made by governments in the Universal Declaration of Human Rights.

 Activity 1 A charter of rights

In groups:

a) Imagine it is the year 2301 and you have been chosen by the President of Earth to be part of a team asked to set up new space colonies throughout the Universe. You have just received the following e-mail, read it carefully and carry out the instructions.

To ...	Reader
Subject	Congratulations!!!

You have been selected by the President of Earth to join a team of experts who will set up a new colony somewhere in the Galaxy. Your first task is to appoint a leader from your group and to decide on a name for your new space colony.

It is very important that all the citizens of your colony feel that they are going to be treated well and that their human rights will be protected. So ... your second task is to write a Human Rights Charter for your colony. To make sure that this is done fairly, follow the instructions below carefully.

* Everyone in the group should call out the human rights that they think the citizens of the colony should have and the leader should write them down. *Remember human rights are things that everyone is entitled to – just because they are human. They don't have to be earned, so think carefully. Here's a few ideas to get you started: Do you think everyone should have a right to a house? Should everyone be able to go to school? Etc.*
* Now discuss and select the top ten human rights on which you all agree.
* Record these on a new piece of paper as your Human Rights Charter.
* Await further instructions from Earth ...

It is now the year 2326 and your Space Colony and their Human Rights Charter have been in operation for about twenty-five years but all is not well in the galaxy. News reports show that some people are not being treated fairly.

NEWSFLASH 1

A local girl has stolen a *Rocket Girl* comic from a shop. She was arrested and taken to jail. News is coming in that one of her fingers has been cut off as punishment.

NEWSFLASH 2 The government announced this morning that only humans from Earth can vote in the upcoming elections. Anyone who has come to live and work on this colony from planets other than Earth will not be allowed to vote no matter how long they or their families have lived here.

NEWSFLASH 3

Government officials found out last night that a group of protestors, who are unhappy with the way the colony is being run, had printed up leaflets and were going to post them to every home in the colony. These leaflets have been found and destroyed and a law is to be passed next week making it illegal for people to write or speak out against the government.

Newsflash 4

It has just been announced that the Interplanetary Church of Zog has been outlawed. Everyone must now join the Intergalactic Church of Chog.

b) Read the newsflashes and discuss the following questions for each to help you evaluate your charter:

- Does anything seem unjust or unfair about this situation?
- What does your Human Rights Charter say on the issue?
- Does your charter need amending? If so, how?

c) Make any changes that you think are necessary to your Human Rights Charter and sign it to show that everyone agrees with its contents.

d) Finally, compare your Human Rights Charter with the charters from other groups.

- What do you all agree on?
- What differences are there?
- What surprised you about each other's charters?
- Can you agree on a combined 'universal' charter for all the colonies?

In topic 18 you found out that all the countries of the world carried out a very similar exercise to the one you have just completed when they drew up the Universal Declaration of Human Rights. By signing the UDHR these countries promised to make sure that the human rights of all people everywhere were protected. So the 30 articles of the UDHR are 30 promises made to the citizens of the world.

 **Activity 2** Researching the rights

a) Research what the articles of the UDHR are. You can find the full declaration and list of articles on the UDHR website.

b) How close were the contents of your Charter to the actual articles of the UDHR?

 **Activity 3**
Personal journal

In your journal write a short paragraph about the promises made by governments to *you* and *all* the citizens of the world in the UDHR. Which ones do you think will be the hardest for governments to keep? Which ones do you think are the most important for governments to keep? Try to write down how you *feel* about the promises made as well as giving some examples of the ones which you think are the most important for you. You could also select one or two of the promises and illustrate them by drawing pictures or cartoons.

In topic 19 you learned about the important promises made by governments to all the citizens of the world. In this topic you will find out about the special promises which have been made to children.

The United Nations Convention on the Rights of the Child

On 20 November 1989 the General Assembly of the United Nations adopted the United Nations Convention on the Rights of the Child (UNCRC). To date almost every country in the world has signed the UNCRC which makes it one of the most widely accepted documents in the world.

The patchwork quilt opposite is a summary of some of the articles from the UNCRC.

 ## Activity 1 Get them sorted!

Children's rights experts have said that the UNCRC contains rights designed to help children to survive and develop, to protect them and to help them play a part in society and have a say. These ideas can be summed up under three headings: provision rights, protection rights and participation rights.

■ Sort each of the articles opposite under these three headings.

■ Record your answers in a table like the one below. Notice how the articles have been summarised. Try to do the same. Also don't worry if some statements suit a couple of categories – just choose what you think is the best.

Provision	Protection	Participation
E.g. right to education	E.g. right to be free from abuse	E.g. right to be listened to

 ## Activity 2 Personal journal

■ Choose, record (and even illustrate) three human rights in the UNCRC which you consider to be the most significant for the children in your community.

■ Repeat this task for each of the groups of children pictured on page 42. What would be their top three rights from the UNCRC?

Articles from the UNCRC

Article 1
Everyone under the age of 18 is a child.

Article 6
Children have the right to life and to survive and develop healthily.

Article 7
Children have the right to a name.

Article 27
Children have the right to a good standard of living.

Article 13
Children have the right to get and share information, as long as it is not damaging to them or others.

Article 14
Children have the right to think and believe what they want.

Article 9
Children should not be separated from their parents unless it is for their own good. If a child's parents are separated then the child should be allowed to see both parents.

Article 15
Children have a right to meet together and form groups or organisations.

Article 12
Children have the right to say what they think should happen to them and to have their opinions taken seriously.

Article 3
Any decision taken about a child must have their 'best interests' at heart.

Article 19
Children should be protected from abuse.

Article 22
Refugee children should have the same rights as children born in the country.

Article 29
Education should be about developing children's personality and talents.

Article 24
Children have the right to good quality health care, and richer countries should help poorer countries to make sure all children all healthy.

Article 30
Children have a right to learn the language (and customs) of their family even if this is not the main language of the country they live in.

Article 33
Children should be protected from dangerous drugs.

Article 23
Children with disabilities should be given special care.

Article 28
Children have the right to an education.

Article 38
Children under 16 years old should not be permitted to join an army or take part in armed conflict.

Article 35
Children should not be sold or abducted.

Article 37
Children who break the law should not be treated cruelly. If a child is put into jail, they should be kept separate from adult prisoners and should have contact with their family.

Article 32
Children should be protected from dangerous work.

Article 31
Children have the right to play.

Article 39
Any child who has been neglected or abused should get special help to make sure that they can live normal lives.

Article 42
Children have a right to learn about these rights.

Article 16
Children have the right to privacy.

Learning intentions

I am learning:

✓ how children's rights are being protected around the world

✓ to research and present findings on how well children's rights are protected in Northern Ireland.

In topic 20 you learned that nearly every country in the world has promised to protect children's rights by signing the UNCRC. However, children around the world are living in dangerous situations where they are not well protected or provided for, or do not have the chance to participate in decisions made that affect them. The photos below show some examples.

Some children are used as soldiers in armed conflicts. These boys fought in the Democratic Republic of Congo.

Many children are affected by famine like this Ethiopian child.

UNICEF is an organisation which has been set up by the United Nations to promote children's rights. In activity 1 you will use their website to find out how well children's rights are being looked after around the world.

 ## Activity 1 Good news ... Bad news ...

In groups:

Imagine you have been asked by UNICEF to produce a short news broadcast about children's rights around the world.

■ Each group member should select a different country and, using UNICEF's website (www.unicef.org), find at least one 'good news' story about children's rights being protected and at least one 'bad news' story about what still needs to be done. *For example, in the Congo there have been no reported cases of polio in recent years because of health programmes, BUT the number of street children is increasing.*

■ Bring all the group's information together and decide on the best way to present your ideas. For example, will you have a reporter interviewing children from the countries? Will it be presented like a studio-based debate?

■ Now present your broadcast to the rest of the class.

Many children are living in poverty and many are neglected. This brother and sister live in Texas, USA.

What is the role of the United Nations?

The United Nations has set up a committee called the Committee on the Rights of the Child. Their job is to make sure that governments keep the promises they have made (or 'comply with the UNCRC'). The UN can send in investigators called 'Special Rapporteurs' to find out if a country is keeping the promises it has made, not just those in the UNCRC but in any convention the country has signed.

A UN Special Rapporteur speaks about the human right to food.

 Activity 2 Children's rights rapporteur

Imagine you are a Special Rapporteur for the UN. You have been asked to produce a report on children's rights in Northern Ireland. You should use the UNCRC as a guide to find out how well children's rights are being protected.

In groups:

a) Select at least five articles from the UNCRC (see page 41) that you think are important rights for children in Northern Ireland.

b) Use these to draw up a list of questions that you want to find out answers to. For example: How good are play facilities for children? How well are children consulted about the decisions that affect them? How good an education do children receive in Northern Ireland? Etc.

c) Now gather information to answer these questions. You could use any of the following sources:

- newspaper extracts
- the Northern Ireland Commissioner for Children and Young People website, where you can find out about the research carried out in Northern Ireland (www.niccy.org)
- interviews with other children in your class
- interviews with adults in your school
- the websites of other organisations such as Barnardos, Save the Children, Children's Law Centre, etc., who campaign for children's rights in Northern Ireland
- invite in speakers from these organisations to your class.

d) Finally, pull all the information together into one report. This should include an overview of your findings and some recommendations about how children's rights could be better protected.

 **Activity 3**
Personal journal

In this topic you have used and developed a wide range of skills such as: managing information, decision making, being creative, self-management and working with others.

a) Choose one of the skills in which you have a particular strength and write a few sentences explaining how you used it in this topic. For example, *I am good at working with others. In this topic I was able to get my own work done and help others too. I also made sure that everyone worked well together in the group.*

b) Choose one of the skills which you think you could develop further and write a few sentences explaining how you could do this in a future topic or in another subject. For example, *I could improve on my decision-making skills. It took me a long time to decide which information was best. In the future I will ask others to help me make decisions more quickly.*

Local and Global Citizenship

Learning intentions

I am learning:
- ✓ about qualities that make a person socially responsible
- ✓ to define the term 'social responsibility'.

Jewish families surrender to Nazi soldiers in 1943.

Activity 1
What is social responsibility?

In pairs:

■ Identify the groups of people who may be treated unfairly in Northern Ireland. Begin by thinking about people whose lives are more difficult than others or people who have special needs or people who may feel left out of society. You might find it useful to look through some local newspapers to help you with this, or by discussing this with your teacher.

■ Select three of these groups and write a modern version of Pastor Niemöller's poem.

First they came ...

First they came for the Communists
And I didn't speak out—
Because I wasn't a Communist.

Then they came for the Jews
And I didn't speak out—
Because I wasn't a Jew.

Then they came for the Trade Unionists
And I didn't speak out—
Because I wasn't a Trade Unionist.

Then they came for the Catholics
And I didn't speak out—
Because I wasn't a Catholic.

Then they came for me—
And by that time no one was left
To speak out for me.

Pastor Martin Niemöller (a German Christian minister who survived a concentration camp).

The poem helps to explain what social responsibility is about. The people mentioned in it were all members of groups or communities who were treated unfairly, simply because they were seen to be 'different' or because they spoke out against unfair laws. The writer felt that he did not act in a socially responsible way because he did not speak out against this persecution and discrimination. Today certain groups are still treated in this way. Some people choose to ignore what happens to others. Other people choose to speak out. Being socially responsible means caring about the rights of others and finding ways to help them to play a full part in our society.

There are many people who are committed to trying to make a difference and being socially responsible. These people have special qualities or characteristics (for example, thoughtfulness, generosity, courage, etc.). Read the following short profiles about some of these people and think about their special qualities.

NAME: William Currie (Local Community Activist, East Belfast)
ACHIEVEMENTS: Campaigned for the rights of older people. He raised money to set up a day centre for older people in his community and to supply groceries and coal for those who could not afford basic necessities. He was awarded the MBE in 1970 for his services to the community.

NAME: Edmund Ignatius Rice (Founder of Christian Brothers' schools in Ireland)
ACHIEVEMENTS: He was a Christian Brother who devoted himself to working with the poor and needy. He gave up his worldly possessions and devoted his life to training teachers who would teach children from poor backgrounds.

NAME: Dr. Houston McKelvey (Clergyman)
ACHIEVEMENTS: He has been involved in voluntary work for most of his life. He is best known as the 'Black Santa', who each year sits out at St Anne's Cathedral, Belfast and collects money which goes to the poor and needy.

NAME: Patricia Hughes (Local Community Activist, West Belfast)
ACHIEVEMENTS: Has spent her life engaged in voluntary community work. In the past, she has helped to build a community centre in her community and now gives up her time to work with Age Concern and to manage a pre-school playgroup.

 Activity 2 What qualities make a person socially responsible?

a) Write down all the words that come into your head to describe the people in the profiles.
b) Choose six words or phrases that you think best describe the qualities that make someone socially responsible.
c) Use these words to create a word search. Swap your word search with your partner and ask them to try to find your words. You should complete your partner's word search too.
d) Finally, work with your partner to produce a definition of the term 'social responsibility' using the ideas in your word searches.

 **Activity 3** Personal journal

Answer the following questions in your journal:

- Is having a sense of social responsibility important?
- How socially responsible am I?
- In what ways could I be more socially responsible?

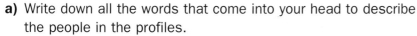

Learning intentions

I am learning:
- ✓ to explore influences on individual identity
- ✓ to define what is meant by individual identity.

Your identity is formed by a number of different things such as your individual likes, dislikes, beliefs, etc. It is also influenced by *groups* that you belong to such as your community, your church, your school, etc. These may affect the religious, cultural and political aspects of your identity. In this topic you will explore how *individual* identity is shaped and expressed. In the following five topics you will explore how *group* identity is shaped, how it is expressed in Northern Ireland and the challenges and opportunities this may bring to your society.

 Activity 1 What influences individual identity?

While we may like to reveal various aspects of our identity, there are certain parts of their identity which a person may choose to keep hidden. This is a bit like an iceberg, which keeps most of its mass below the surface of the sea.

Individually:

a) Draw an iceberg on a sheet of paper and mark on a water line (quite close to the top). Think about what aspects of identity are immediately visible or which people might be willing to show, for example gender, age, ethnic background, disabilities, etc. Record these on your iceberg *above* the water line – you could write, draw or use cuttings or photographs to record different aspects.

b) Think about what aspects of identity are *not* immediately visible or which people are *not* willing to show, for example nationality, sexuality or even some of the examples given in part a). Record these on the iceberg *below* the water line.

c) There may be some aspects of identity which some people are willing to show but which others are not willing to show, for example name, hobbies and interests, religion, political beliefs. Decide where you think they should go too.

As a class:

d) Compare your iceberg with those from the rest of your class.

e) Discuss with the rest of the class why some people choose to keep certain things about their individual identity hidden in Northern Ireland, and try to produce a combined 'Identity Iceberg' showing the opinion of the whole class.

Activity 2 Defining individual identity

This activity will help you to define what is meant by individual identity.

In groups:

a) Get a large piece of paper and draw a line from one side of it to the other. Label one end 'Strongly Agree' and label the other 'Strongly Disagree'. In the middle of the line write 'Not Sure'.

b) Discuss each of the statements about identity written on the cards below and decide where you would place it along the line. Record the card number on the appropriate place on your line.

c) Compare your answers with the rest of the class.

- What did you all agree on?
- What did you disagree on?
- What surprised you?

d) Use the feedback and some of the ideas on the cards to agree a definition of 'individual identity'.

1 | Where I live has an influence on who I am.

2 | **Identity is something that changes as I get older.**

3 | *I feel that I sometimes have to hide parts of my identity.*

4 | Identity is part choice and part decided for you.

5 | *My religious beliefs are central to my sense of identity.*

6 | *Identity is not linked to the colour of my skin.*

7 | **I sometimes give up bits of my identity to please certain people.**

8 | I can express my identity by the clothes I wear.

9 | *I cannot see how language is linked to identity.*

 # Activity 3
Personal journal

Use the following questions to reflect on your own identity:

- What do you understand by the term 'identity'?
- What aspects of your identity are you willing to share with everyone?
- What aspects of your identity are you *not* willing to share with everyone?

Local and Global Citizenship

A long time ago a man called John Donne famously wrote these words:

'No man is an island, entire of itself; every man is a piece of the continent, a part of the main.'

What Donne meant by these words was that each of us as individuals cannot live alone, we are far more closely connected to other people than we may think. In Northern Ireland today, people rarely live in isolation. Instead we become part of groups and live as members of communities (in 'common unity'). The groups we belong to are sometimes as a result of our own choice, but we can also be born into different groups too. Can you think of a few examples of these?

In topic 23 you discovered that there are areas of identity that are quite individual and personal to each and every one of us. There are also aspects of identity that we share with others, like our support of football teams, religious beliefs and our age. We express this group identity in a number of ways, for example the language we use, the traditions we keep, the customs we follow, the possessions we cherish. Quite often we use symbols, colours, clothing, badges and flags, etc. as a way of connecting or associating ourselves to certain groups. These types of items are sometimes called 'cultural artefacts'.

 Activity 1 What artefacts do we use to express our cultural identity?

Imagine you have been asked to organise a time capsule for your community, which will be used to inform the people of the future about the cultural aspects of your life today.

In groups:

a) Decide what would be the significant artefacts and items that you would place into such a time capsule.

b) Repeat this activity to decide what would go in a time capsule for *all* of Northern Ireland:

- How would it differ from your community's time capsule?
- How would it be similar?
- Could any of the artefacts or items cause offence or present challenges to people in our society?

Activity 2 How do we use music and song to express identity?

Music has always been an important way to express both individual and group identity.

Individually:

a) Think about some of your favourite songs.

b) Write down your three favourites and answer the following questions.

- What are they about?
- What do the lyrics say?
- What do you like about the song?

In pairs:

c) Share your thoughts with a partner. Do these songs unite you? Why? Why not?

d) Pair up again and share your thoughts within a group of four.

e) Next, think about how some songs and music can divide different groups of people in Northern Ireland.

- Do you ever feel uncomfortable about some songs or types of music?
- Do you sing any of these types of songs yourself?

f) Share your group's thoughts with the whole class and record examples of how songs can be used to unite or to divide different groups in Northern Irish society.

 # Activity 3 Can some songs be offensive?

Imagine a new local radio station 'Diverse FM' has opened. They want you to check their play list will appeal to all members of the community. Your task is to research the lyrics of the songs on the CD cover on the right and answer these questions:

- Why do some people identify strongly with these songs?
- Why might some people find these songs threatening?
- Should these songs be played on Diverse FM?

You can research the lyrics of these songs by typing the song title and the word 'lyrics' into Google (www.google.co.uk) and running a search (e.g. 'God Save the Queen lyrics').

 # Activity 4
Personal journal

Design a playlist of up to ten songs that you would include on a MP3 playlist called 'My cultural identity'. Write them in your journal and briefly explain what the music expresses about who you are. You might like to think about whether the music says something about you religiously, politically or culturally and if so, what?

1 God save the Queen
2 The Boys of the Old Brigade
3 The Men Behind the Wire
4 The Soldiers Song
5 Four Green Fields
6 Celtic Symphony
7 The Billy Boys
8 Green Fields of France

WHAT IS SECTARIANISM?

Learning intentions

I am learning:

✓ to explore the meaning of the term sectarianism

✓ to discuss the causes and consequences of sectarianism in Northern Ireland.

Sectarianism showing strong commitment to a particular religion and rejecting others who do not share your belief;

prejudice or discrimination against people with a different religious or cultural background;

acting on stereotypes of a religious group.

In topic 24 you explored how groups in Northern Ireland express their identity. You also thought about some of the problems or challenges associated with this. In this chapter you will explore one of those challenges: sectarianisim.

Defining sectarianism

What exactly do we mean by the term 'sectarianism'? On the left are some dictionary definitions.

Some of these definitions use words that you may be unsure of but the three main words that turn up when talking about sectarianism are:

1 stereotype
2 prejudice
3 discrimination.

Put simply ...

- A stereotype is a generalisation about a group of people that isn't altogether true, e.g. 'all girls are giggly'.
- Prejudice is making judgements about people (pre-judging) based on stereotypes, e.g. 'that wee girl is bound to be all giggly and it'll really annoy me'.
- Discrimination is taking unfair action against someone because of the group they belong to, e.g. 'no girls are allowed to join our club'.

So while they all have different meanings you can see how they are connected to each other.

Cause and consequences of sectarianism

Sectarianism, particularly in Northern Ireland, has meant that many people from the two main communities here (Catholic/ Protestant or Nationalist/Unionist) do not have many opportunities to mix with each other. It's almost like sectarianism has built a wall between people in Northern Ireland. In fact during the worst period of the conflict here (or the 'Troubles' as some people call it) actual walls, called 'peacelines' were built to keep communities separate from each other.

A 'peaceline' in West Belfast, in 1988.

Activity 1 Wall of sectarianism

Individually:

a) Copy the picture of the wall opposite into your journal and write onto each of the bricks some words which you think help you to understand the term 'sectarianism'. Some have already been done to help you, and the speech bubbles below should also give you some ideas.

In groups:

b) Show your walls to each other and then use your ideas to try to write your own description of sectarianism and its causes and consequences. You can use this template as a guide:

'Sectarianism is............. It happens when.........
Its result are.......'

People
who are sectarian think
they are right and
everyone else is wrong –
it's really narrow-minded.

People
who are sectarian really
don't know enough about 'the
other side'. They believe a lot of
lies about the other community
and never try to find out
the truth.

Sectarianism
is when you treat someone
differently because of their
religious and political
beliefs.

Sectarianism
is very complicated – it's
not just about religion ...
it's about people not
respecting your culture
and traditions.

A lot of
people here think they're not
sectarian ... but I think
everyone here is a bit
bigotted whether they want to
admit it or not.

Tackling sectarianism

There are many ways that sectariansim in Northern Ireland can be, and has been, challenged by individuals, society and the government. For example, as long ago as the 1970s *individual* teachers started bringing school children together from the two main communities to learn more about each other and to help them think about some of the prejudiced attitudes they may have held. Organisations, like the Community Relations Council, have been set up in *society* to try to tackle sectarianism and efforts have also been made to 'kick sectarianism out' of football. The *government* has also tried to deal with the issue by promoting good relations between the two main communities but also by writing laws that make it illegal to discriminate against someone because of their religious or political opinion.

 # Activity 2
Personal journal

Think about the different ways people in Northern Ireland are trying to tackle sectarianism. Choose one example that you think *you* could get involved in either now or when you are older. Imagine you are a lot older and reflecting on what you did get involved in. Write a short letter, in your journal, to your 'future grandchild' explaining what you did, why you did it and what difference you think it made.

Learning intentions

I am learning:

✓ to define what is meant by 'diversity'

✓ to present information about ethnic diversity in Northern Ireland.

Northern Ireland is an increasingly diverse community. This means that there are many differences between the people who live here. The images below show that there is a wide range of people from different ethnic backgrounds living in Northern Ireland. Some have decided to come and live here while others were born here. This ethnic diversity brings new and exciting things to our community.

 Activity 1 Celebrating diversity!

Imagine you have been asked to design a PowerPoint® presentation for Community Relations Week called 'Celebrating Ethnic Diversity in Northern Ireland'.

In groups:

a) Decide what would make a successful presentation. For example, clearly presented information, colourful slides, interesting images, etc.

b) Share these ideas with the rest of the class and draw up a list of 'success criteria' for this activity.

c) In your group, use the images to the left and your own knowledge, to list as many of the different ethnic communities in Northern Ireland as you can.

d) Each member of your group should choose a community to research, and find out about their religious beliefs, cultural traditions, food and drink, sport, music, dance, etc, in order to produce at least one slide for the group presentation. You can use these weblinks to gather the information:

- www.bbc.co.uk/northernireland/schools
- www.workingwithdiversity.org/div/racialgroup/index.php

e) Bring your slides together as a group and add an introduction slide and a conclusion slide:

- An introduction slide should explain what is meant by ethnic diversity and give an overview of the range of ethnic communities in Northern Ireland.
- A conclusion slide should give examples of how our society has been enriched by ethnic diversity.

f) Share your presentation with the rest of the class and ask them to assess your group's performance using the success criteria you decide as a class.

g) Individually:
Summarise what you have learned about ethnic diversity using, for example, a spider diagram, bullet point notes, a table, etc.

Who works on behalf of ethnic minority communities?

As well as government organisations, like the Equality Commission, there are many NGOs (Non-Governmental Organisations) that work for the benefit of people from ethnic minority communities who live in Northern Ireland. These organisations help by speaking out on behalf of ethnic minority communities, providing support services and making sure that their human rights are protected.

ORGANISATION: Community Relations Council
WEBSITE: www.community-relations.org.uk
While the main work of the CRC is to promote good relations between the two main communities in Northern Ireland they are also involved in promoting inclusion for ethnic minority groups. Amongst other things, they provide funding for projects which support good relations. They also provide training and support services and publish information leaflets and educational materials to raise awareness about diversity.

ORGANISATION: An Munia Tober
WEBSITE: www.anmuniatober.org
This is a Traveller support group which works towards making sure that Travellers in Belfast have access to all the services they need and are seen as equal citizens in society. They run projects with Travellers on such issues as health, education, play, youth work and cultural heritage.

ORGANISATION: Northern Ireland Council for Ethnic Minorities (NICEM)
WEBSITE: www.nicem.org.uk
NICEM supports people from ethnic minority communities in Northern Ireland. They help people set up community groups, raise awareness of issues that affect ethnic minority communities, and provide an interpreting service for people who do not speak English. NICEM offers support to people who have been bullied or attacked because they are different. NICEM also tries to ensure that laws do not exclude or have a negative effect on the needs of ethnic minority communities.

Activity 2 Supporting ethnic minority communities

Individually:
a) Read the fact files above which will give you information about the NGOs who support ethnic minority communities in Northern Ireland.
b) Now copy and complete this table to summarise the information. You could add in other organisations, perhaps from your local area.

Name of group	What community (ies) does this organisation serve?	What things does this organisation do?
NICEM		
Community Relations Council		
An Munia Tober		

Activity 3
Personal journal

a) Imagine what it would be like in Northern Ireland if there were no ethnic minority communities living here. What would you miss? Record your thoughts using single words, phrases, images and symbols against a background of a map of Northern Ireland.
b) Now think about how your life is richer because of the diversity that exists in our society. Record your thoughts again using single words, phrases, images and symbols against a new background of a map of Northern Ireland.

Local and Global Citizenship

Learning intentions

I am learning:

✓ to explain the term racism
✓ to evaluate how racism is being tackled by individuals, society and government.

Racism in Northern Ireland

The following report was aired on BBC News in 2000 and was based on a government-funded report which questioned 1250 people (it has been adapted here):

> Racial attacks are on the increase in Northern Ireland. ... Two-thirds of those questioned said they would not work with Travellers. More than half would not accept Travellers as neighbours. More than a third of those polled said they would not like to work with Asian, Afro-Caribbean or Chinese people. A quarter said they could not accept members of these ethnic groups as neighbours. However, 83 per cent of the people polled said they supported the need for effective equal opportunities policies for ethnic minority people. And 87 per cent felt that children should be taught about minority ethnic peoples' traditions in school.

 ## Activity 1 In the news

a) Read the news broadcast carefully and answer the following questions:

■ Which ethnic minority groups are mentioned in the report? Write a list.
■ How many people said they would work with Travellers?
■ How many said they would not accept Asian, Chinese or Afro-Carribean people as neighbours?

b) Later on, the report used the words 'prejudice' and 'racism'. Write down your own definition for each of these words.

c) Did anything in the report surprise you? If so, what?

d) At the end of the broadcast it mentioned two ways of tackling racism: laws and policies to help ethnic minority groups and educating young people about ethnic minority traditions. How do you think these suggestions might help?

e) Can you think of any other ways individuals, society and government could tackle racism?

The consequence of racism

Look at the consequence wheel on page 55. It has been completed to show how one single racist incident can have a huge impact. The centre of the wheel describes a racist incident. The next 'ring' gives three immediate consequences of this. The outer ring shows two 'knock-on' consequences for each of the immediate ones – a bit like a ripple effect.

Activity 2 Consequence wheel

In groups:

a) Make a blank copy of the consequence wheel.

b) Think about the immediate and 'knock-on' consequences of the following example of racism: 'Pregnant Portuguese woman suffers attack and verbal abuse in town centre'.

c) Complete the wheel for this incident by recording your ideas.

d) Repeat this activity for another incident you may have heard about or read about (or search the BBC news website).

e) Display all the consequence wheels in your class. Use them to identify and list the main types of consequences of racism, for example financial cost, emotional cost, etc.

f) Give examples from the consequence wheels for each type of consequence you have listed.

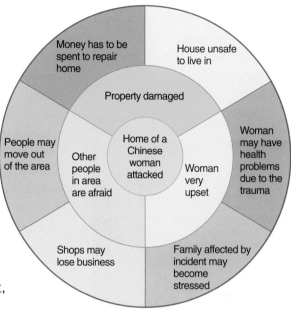

Consequence wheel

This activity shows that racism has consequences for *individuals* and their families (upset, pain, financial costs, etc.) and for *society* as a whole (impact on businesses, community safety, community relations and even the cost of policing incidents, etc.).

Challenging racism

There are some good examples of ways in which people have tried to tackle racism here and in other parts of the world. Many of their strategies are aimed at young people like you in schools as the following examples show.

Show Racism the Red Card is part of the FARE (Football Against Racism in Europe) network. It uses professional footballers as anti-racist role models and aims to combat racism through anti-racist education.

www.srtrc.org

Britkid is a website that explores ethnic diversity in the UK. It allows people to gain a greater understanding of the traditions and customs of other communities as well as tackling the issues of racism.

www.britkid.org

 # Activity 3
Tackling racism

In your groups:
Choose one of the organisations mentioned on the left. Visit their website and choose one of their resources or ideas to design a short (ten minute) lesson on 'Tackling Racism' for the rest of your class. You will then have to teach this lesson to your class!

 # Activity 4
Personal journal

Reflect on all the activities in this topic and complete the following sentences:

- I have learned that racism is …
- I think racism can be tackled by …
- I have contributed to this class by …

Local and Global Citizenship

Learning intentions

I am learning:

✓ about how I depend on the rest of the world
✓ to define the term 'diversity'.

Martin Luther King (Jnr) speaks about racial discrimination at a news conference in 1963.

The last few topics have helped you to recognise that Northern Ireland is a diverse society. However, we also need to remember that we are only one small part of the whole world. If we are to be able to appreciate diversity on a global scale then we need to learn about other countries and their cultures.

Learning about other societies can help us to challenge the types of stereotypes and prejudices we have been exploring in the last few topics. It also helps us realise how much we depend on one another – this is called interdependence.

Martin Luther King (Jnr) was a famous civil rights activist who fought against racial discrimination in the United States of America. He was committed to protecting the human rights of everyone regardless of their ethnic background and was dedicated to encouraging everyone to consider how they depend on one another. This quote from him explains the idea of interdependence really well:

> 'You get up in the morning and go to the bathroom and reach over for the sponge, and that's handed to you by a Pacific islander. You reach for a bar of soap, and that's given to you at the hands of a Frenchman. And then you go into the kitchen to drink your coffee for the morning, and that's poured into your cup by a South American. And then you reach over for your toast, and that's given to you at the hands of an English-speaking farmer, not to mention the baker. And before you finish eating breakfast in the morning, you've depended on more than half the world.'

The quote shows that we are all connected to each other no matter how far we may live apart or no matter how different our backgrounds may be. Just as in topic 26 you recognised that our lives are richer in Northern Ireland because of the different ethnic minority communities living here, our lives are also richer because of the global diversity that exists in our world and the access we have to it. The following activities will help you to reflect on how you depend on the rest of the world and the importance of diversity in your life.

Activity 1
Before finishing breakfast ...

a) How many different types of people from around the world did Martin Luther King (Jnr) say he depended on before he finished his breakfast?

b) Write down all the products he said he used from around the world.

c) Do you agree with the last sentence of the quote or not? Explain your answer.

Activity 2 Connecting the world

a) Individually, think about your life. How many other countries do you depend on? What countries have an influence on:

- the food you eat
- the clothes you wear (just look at the labels!)
- the sports you enjoy
- the music you listen to
- the TV programmes you watch?

b) Copy the spider diagram below and complete it to show how you depend on the rest of the world.

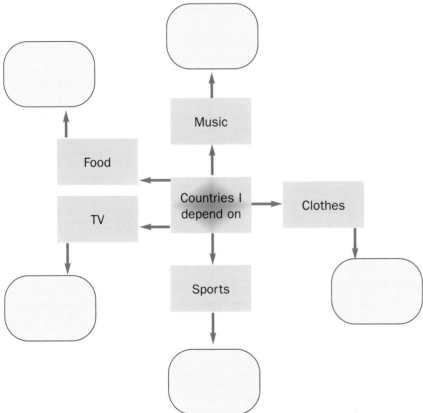

 # Activity 3 Celebrating diversity

a) In groups:
Design a patchwork quilt to illustrate diversity in Northern Ireland and to celebrate the positive aspects of a diverse society.

b) Each square of the quilt should illustrate a different aspect of diversity in Northern Ireland.

c) You can use some of the images and symbols from the other topics or some of the ideas and words you have recorded in your journal.

 # Activity 4
Defining diversity

By now you should have a good idea about what diversity means. Individually, record your ideas in an acrostic poem using the letters of the word 'diversity' to start each new line. An example has been started for you:

Differences are all around us
In everything we do and say
Variety enriches our community
Every single day
R …
S …
I …
T …
Y …

 # Activity 5
Personal journal

In your journal design your own personal patchwork quilt. Place a square in the middle that represents you. Design the other squares using the symbols and ideas you have been looking at in the last few topics. Place these symbols close to your square in the centre if they are important to you or further out if they are less important.

Learning intentions

I am learning:

✓ to identify the things I have in common with my fellow students and those things that make me different

✓ to investigate and evaluate how inclusive my school really is.

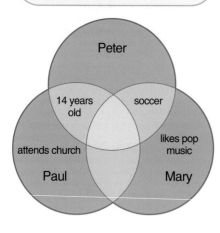

Have you ever heard anyone say something like, 'Young people! Sure they're all the same, aren't they!'? Hopefully, you will disagree with this statement and by now will have recognised that we are all very different.

 Activity 1 How diverse is my class?

a) Individually:

Answer the following questions.

1 Do you have any religious beliefs? If so, what are they?
2 Do you like sport? If so, which sports do you follow?
3 What age are you?
4 What type of music do you like or dislike?
5 What traditions do you follow?
6 What are your favourite foods?
7 What kind of a neighbourhood do you live in?
8 Do you have any special needs at school (e.g. dietary)?
9 How would you describe your nationality?
10 Do you have any political beliefs?

b) In a group of three, draw three overlapping circles on a page. Label the circles with the names of your group members (like the diagram opposite).

c) Discuss your answer for question 1 with the rest of the group. Do you have the same answer as anyone else in your group? If so, record it in the overlapping parts of your circles. If not, record it in the part of the circle that does not overlap.

d) Repeat this for the rest of the questions.

e) Once you have completed all ten use your diagram to answer this question: 'How diverse is my group?' Identify the main ways you are alike and the main ways you are different to help you answer.

f) Report back your findings to the rest of the class and listen to the findings of the other groups. Now answer the question: 'How diverse is my class?'

Understanding that people are different in terms of age, skin colour, ethnicity, gender, beliefs, ability, etc. can help us all to create a more inclusive society. Your school should provide a caring, welcoming and inclusive environment for everyone in the community that it serves. So let's ask the question: how inclusive is your school?

 Activity 2 How inclusive is my school?

a) In groups:

Copy out the report card on page 59 (make it larger where necessary).

b) Discuss each statement and try to find evidence for your view.

c) Record this evidence on the report card and give your school a mark out of three (see scorecard).

d) Ask your teacher to help you with any bit you find difficult or where you are unsure about the evidence.

SCORECARD

If you find plenty of evidence to support the statement, score your school 3 points. **= 3**

If you find some evidence to support the statement, score your school 2 points. **= 2**

If you find little or no evidence to support the statement, score your school 1 point. **= 1**

SCHOOL REPORT

Name of school: _____

Diversity and Inclusion Audit

	Evidence	Score
1 Our school accepts students of all abilities.		
2 Our school values and respects the opinions and views of its students.		
3 Our school sees its students as individuals and helps them to learn in ways that meet their individual needs.		
4 Our school provides support for students with special needs.		
5 Our school has good access for wheelchair users.		
6 Our school welcomes students from all communities.		
7 Our school welcomes students from different ethnic and language backgrounds.		
8 Our school offers a range of subjects and opportunities that allow students to participate in a diverse range of activities.		
9 Our school accepts students of all faiths.		
10 Our school accepts both boys and girls.		
11 Our school provides a diverse range of food in the canteen.		
12 Our school writes down its belief in diversity in various documents, e.g. website, prospectus, etc.		
Final Report (write in your final outcomes and recommendations)		**Total**

So, how well is our school doing?

25–36 = High Fliers!! Our school is really inclusive and welcoming.

13–24 = Preparing to take off! Our school is quite good, but there may be room for improvement.

0–12 = We're in big trouble! Our school has a lot of work to do. Could do better!

Activity 3
Taking it further

Now that you have audited your school, you may have identified some aspects of your school which could better cater for diversity. Think about how you or others could make these improvements happen. Outline your suggestions and present your ideas. For example, you may wish to write a letter to some of your teachers, provide a report to your Principal, prepare a special assembly on diversity and inclusion, or even contact your student council about your findings.

Local and Global Citizenship

Learning intentions

I am learning:

✓ to connect together the ideas I have learned in Local and Global Citizenship

✓ to reflect on the knowledge I have gained and the skills I have developed.

In topic 16 you discovered that Local and Global Citizenship was based on four key themes. You have explored two of those themes over the last fourteen chapters. It is important to note that many of the ideas you have looked at this year will surface again next year. For example you will be using words like stereotype, prejudice and discrimination when you look at 'equality' next year. You will be finding out more about the Universal Declaration of Human Rights and the United Nations Convention on the Rights of the Child too, especially when you are looking at 'social justice'. The themes in Local and Global Citizenship are interconnected. You probably won't really see the big picture until the very end of the course. This topic will give you the opportunity to consolidate (firm up) what you have learned this year so you can build on this next year. Look below at some of the things you've learned about and use these to complete activity 1.

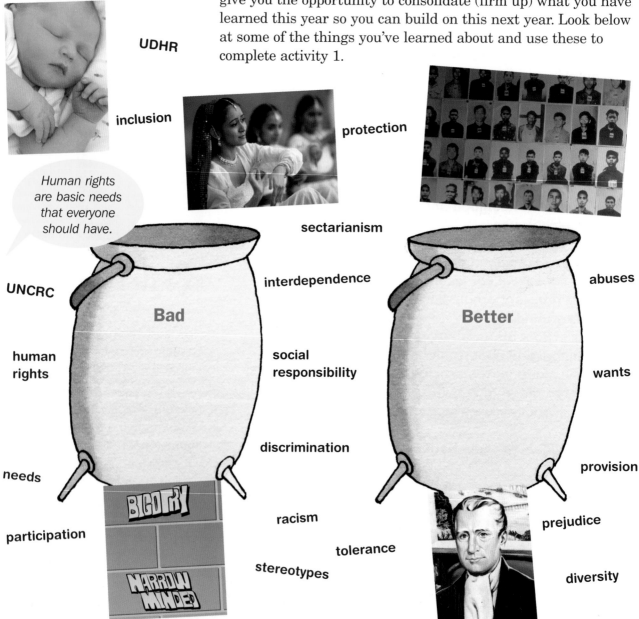

UDHR

inclusion

protection

Human rights are basic needs that everyone should have.

sectarianism

interdependence

abuses

UNCRC

Bad

Better

human rights

social responsibility

wants

needs

discrimination

provision

BIGOTRY

participation

racism

prejudice

tolerance

stereotypes

NARROW MINDED

diversity

Activity 1 Recipes for citizenship

a) In groups:
Draw two big cooking pots onto a large page and label them 'Bad' and 'Better'.

b) Choose symbols and words from page 60, or your own ideas, and decide whether or not they should go into the pot that represents a 'Bad' society or the pot that represents a 'Better' society.

c) Write down and draw your decisions in each of the pots.

d) Use your ideas to write a recipe for a *bad* society (e.g. 'Take a lot of bigotry and add a spoonful of violence', etc) and a recipe for a better society (e.g. 'Take a litre of diversity and stir in some tolerance', etc) beside each pot.

e) Discuss in your group what would need to be done by individuals, society and the government to change the bad recipe into a better recipe! You will get some ideas from topics 25 and 27. Record these ideas on arrows between your two pots.

f) Share your ideas with rest of the class.

 # Activity 2 Personal journal

Local and Global Citizenship is about gaining new knowledge about important issues, developing skills that you can use to make a difference in society and acting on these skills. It's also about challenging your views and the views of others. It can be summed up as knowing, feeling and doing!

On the right is an example of how someone might reflect on their experience of Local and Global Citizenship. Copy the outline of the table into your journal and use it to help you to reflect on your own work over the last fifteen topics and to assess your own learning.

	Knowing	Feeling	Doing
Before exploring these topics ...	I knew a bit about sectarianism but nothing about human rights.	I didn't really have many opinions about any of these issues.	I was confident about talking out in class but I never would've thought of doing a presentation.
Now ...	I know a lot more about human rights and have learned that other countries have problems too.	I feel quite strongly about some of the conditions children live in around the world.	I feel a bit more confident about presenting and I think I'm better at group work.
I would like to ...	Find out more about human rights.	Feel I could make a difference.	Speak to someone in politics about how I feel.

Learning intentions

I am learning:

✓ to recognise that there are a large variety of jobs

✓ to consider what is important to me in a job.

'A job is a paid position of regular or casual employment doing a particular type of work from which a career path may develop.'

The world of work is changing very quickly. You may end up doing a job not even thought of yet. Education for Employability will help you to prepare for the future so that you can make the right choices and be a good employee.

This topic introduces you to the idea that there are many different types of job available, sometimes within the same industry or place of work, and asks you to start thinking about what is important to you in a job.

In Northern Ireland retailing is the biggest employer. For example, in 2005 Tesco employed 8510 people, but they were not all working at the checkout …

Activity 1 More than one job

In pairs:

a) List all the jobs shown opposite that are available in a large supermarket.

b) Can you think of any more? If so add them to your list.

c) Supermarkets don't just employ people in store. Research what other jobs and careers are available by going to their websites (e.g. www.tesco.com, www.sainsburys.co.uk). Find at least five more jobs and add them to your list.

d) Share your list with the rest of the class and make a full class list.

e) What has this activity shown you about the world of work?

In many workplaces or businesses there is a whole range of people doing different jobs with different roles. For example, you cannot assume that everyone working in a school is a teacher. There are also likely to be secretaries, cleaners, caretakers, cooks, a nurse, a bursar, etc.

 # Activity 2 Who works in a place like this?

In pairs:

a) Choose one of the following places of employment and design a poster to show all the different jobs you would find if you opened the doors of that building. Fold your page to make doors and show the building on the outside and the jobs on the inside. You could choose from:

■ a hospital
■ a hotel
■ a builder's yard
■ an airport
■ an idea of your own.

b) Display the posters around the room at the end to make a mini town so you can see all the jobs your class has thought of.

You have probably all been asked, 'What do you want to be when you grow up?' You may not know yet but activity 3 should start you thinking about what might be important to you in a job.

 # Activity 3
Ladders

a) What sorts of things are important to you in your dream job?

■ Draw a ladder like the one above.

■ On each step write something that you think would be important to you in a job. Put the least important on the bottom rung up to the most important on the top rung so that they are in rank order.

■ Here are some things you might consider but you may also have lots of your own ideas to add.

✳ Lots of money ✳ Enjoying my work ✳ Travelling ✳ Expensive car ✳ Smart clothes ✳ Meeting people ✳ Good holidays ✳ Feeling successful ✳ Helping people ✳ Being my own boss

b) In groups compare what your ladder looks like. Are the same things important to all of you?

Skills are something you have learned to do well. They are things you CAN DO.

For example: write neatly, score goals, word process on a computer, tell the time.

Qualities are personal characteristics, things about your personality.

They are things you ARE. For example: caring, determined, hardworking, funny!

Learning intentions

I am learning:

✓ to understand the difference between a quality and a skill
✓ to identify the qualities and skills required for a particular job
✓ to negotiate with others in my class to agree on a list of skills and qualities.

 Activity 1 Skills and qualities

As a class:

Brainstorm lots of words and phrases to describe people and the things they can do. Decide if they are qualities or skills and sort them into a list of each.

Different jobs require different skills and qualities. During the next few years you will make some very important decisions about the type of work you want to do. In order to make good choices you should identify the sort of qualities and skills needed for a particular job. For example, you may think teachers need to have patience, or a builder needs a good head for heights.

Consider some of the skills and qualities a nurse needs.

I can	I am
Follow instructions ←	→ A good listener
Take temperatures ←	→ Caring
Administer medicine ←	→ Trustworthy
Bandage a wound ←	→ Friendly
Sew stitches in a wound ←	→ Hardworking
Work under pressure ←	→ Well-presented
Give injections ←	

Education for Employability

By identifying the qualities and skills required for certain jobs you can make a better judgement about how well a job would suit you. You can start to think about the type of job you would like to do in order to see if it matches the qualities and skills you already have and identify any you might need to develop. (You will find out ways to do this in topic 33.)

 ## Activity 2 I am and I can

In pairs:

a) Look at the people on the right. For each person write the name of their job in the centre of the page and put a column on either side (like the example of the nurse opposite). Title one column 'I can' (skills) and the other column 'I am' (qualities).

HAIRDRESSER

I CAN (skills)	I AM (qualities)

b) In each column list as many skills and qualities as you can that each person might need to do their job well. You could use the lists you made in activity 1 and the example of the nurse on page 64 to help you.

c) Choose a job you would like to do and list the skills and qualities you would need.

 ## Activity 3 The perfect pupil

a) In pairs:
  - Discuss the skills and qualities you think the perfect pupil would have.
  - Make a list of these under the two different headings 'skills' and 'qualities'.
  - Agree on the five most important qualities and five most important skills.
  - Share your list with the rest of the class.

b) As a class:
  - Negotiate and agree the top five skills and top five qualities a perfect pupil should have from the lists everyone has made.
  - Display this list in the class as a reminder.

c) Now have a class discussion on the skills of a perfect teacher, if you dare!

A hairdresser

An architect

A fire-fighter

A lawyer

Learning intentions

I am learning:

✓ to identify my personal qualities and skills
✓ about opportunities in school to develop new qualities and skills.

In topic 32 you looked at qualities and skills needed for different jobs. This topic gives you the opportunity to identify your own qualities and skills. This may help you to decide on the type of job you would like to do, or identify the skills you need to develop in order to pursue the career you are interested in.

But how do you know what your qualities and skills are? With some people it is very obvious what these are.

Activity 1
Claim to fame

In pairs:

a) Discuss what the people in each photograph do and why you think they are so successful at their job.

b) Identify three skills and three qualities they might have which help explain why they are successful at their job. Give reasons for your choice.

Wayne Rooney, footballer

Angelina Jolie, actress

Ant & Dec, TV presenters

Most people, however, find it difficult to identify their own qualities and skills. Yet you are constantly displaying and developing new skills and qualities in the everyday tasks you do.

Activity 2 What about me?

a) Siobhan is a Year 8 pupil. Her form teacher has asked her to list the skills and qualities she has. Siobhan thinks she doesn't have any so her teacher suggests she thinks carefully about some of the things she did over the last few weeks. Look at some of Siobhan's activities (1–6). Can you match them with the words listed below? Give reasons for your choices explaining how her actions display or develop that particular quality or skill.

- Good communicator
- Patient
- Trustworthy
- Well-presented
- Team worker
- Punctual

b) Draw a table like the one below and fill it in matching some of your activities to skills and qualities. Don't forget each activity may develop or show more than one quality or skill.

Activity	Quality/Skill

Hopefully this activity has shown you just how many qualities and skills you have already. Each year you should review your qualities and skills and identify the new ones you have developed.

 **Activity 3**
What an opportunity

School is an excellent place for developing new skills, qualities, making friends and having fun at the same time.

a) As a class, brainstorm all the after school clubs and extra curricular activities there are in your school.

b) In groups, choose one of these and use your IT skills to make a notice which would encourage pupils to participate in that activity.

Show pupils the qualities and skills they can develop by taking part.

These could make a great display around the school for open night, or in a booklet for new pupils.

1

2

3

4

5

6

Learning intentions

I am learning:

✓ to increase my awareness of different types of transferable skills

✓ to understand the skills and qualities employers are looking for.

In topic 33 you looked at qualities and skills. In this topic we will look closely at the type of skills that are transferable. But what are transferable skills?

Skills can be transferred from one job to another. If you train for one type of work you may not end up doing this for the rest of your working life, but many of the skills you learn in one job could be used elsewhere. These are called 'transferable skills'. Transferable skills include skills such as literacy, numeracy and ICT. Other examples include the following:

Working with others

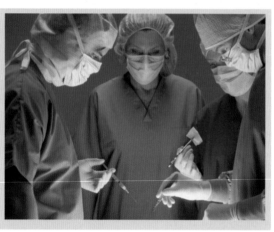

The ability to work effectively as part of a team is an important skill. Most employers would look for evidence of you being able to do this.

Self-management

Self-management is the ability to drive yourself in order to achieve a personal goal and to work independently.

Time management

Employers will expect you to arrive for work on time. If you are continually late for school then this trend is generally carried into the workplace.

Pride in good workmanship

Pride in your work is important in the workplace, as your employer needs to be confident that the job will be done to a high standard.

Activity 1 Time to change

Ken is a builder but wants a change. In his current job he has gained experience in new build and repair work. He has worked with other tradesmen (such as plumbers and electricians) and professionals (such as architects and engineers). He has also had to keep his customers and clients happy.

In pairs:

- Discuss what skills and qualities might be needed for the job advert on the right. Are any of these transferable skills?
- Is Ken qualified to apply for the job? Give reasons why the skills he already has could be transferred and used in this job.
- What does this activity show you about the importance of having transferable skills?

Council Building Inspector

Do you have experience in CONSTRUCTION WORK? Are you willing to negotiate with clients during planning, construction and completion of house alterations?

If so you could become part of a successful council service. The person appointed must have:

- a proven record of experience within the construction industry
- experience of reading plans/drawings
- awareness of current building regulations
- good communication, literacy and numeracy skills
- a clean driving licence.

 # Activity 2 Famous people and their transferable skills

List the skills that you think the following people needed in their original job and have now transferred into their current job.

Eamonn Holmes (Journalist and TV Broadcaster)

Gary Lineker (Professional Footballer and Sports Commentator)

May Blood (Trade Union Representative and Peace Campaigner)

 # Activity 3 Personal journal

Transferable skill	Jobs where I would use this skill
Communication	
ICT	
Literacy skills	
Numeracy skills	
Presentation skills	

Copy and complete the table on the left to compile a list of jobs where transferable skills taught in school would be desirable/required.

Learning intentions

I am learning:

✓ how being enterprising can make you more effective
✓ how to identify what could be changed in daily life to make a day more effective.

Enterprise has been defined as 'Being bold, resourceful and energetic in any attempted task or project'.

Have you ever thought 'I wish I had done it like that!' when you have seen someone do something difficult? For example, you might have admired how a friend carried out an activity in class. Being enterprising is about being able to approach tasks in a more effective way and to continually think about how something could be done better. It is another transferable skill that employers look for. Let's try it for a household task.

Activity 1
The weekly shop

- Look at Erinn's situation on the right.
- Write down the steps she needs to take to complete her shopping.
- Now look at each of these steps – can you think of different ways of completing them in order to give Erinn more free time? (Tip – think about other ways of shopping.)

Situation

Erinn is always rushed off her feet. She has a full-time job and also plays in a hockey team on Saturdays. She has very little time for shopping but has to make sure there is enough food in the house for the week. At the moment she goes shopping on a Sunday – the only time when she doesn't have something else to do! She makes a list, drives to the supermarket and does the shopping. The queues are always bad on a Sunday so the whole trip takes her about an hour and a half.
She would much prefer to be doing something else on her Sundays off!

In activity 1 you started to think about an everyday task and how to act in an enterprising way to carry it out. Why do you think this is a transferable skill employers look for?

Activity 2 Organising the day

Look at an average day for Tom, a twelve-year-old schoolboy.

Tom sleeps as long as he can until he is told to get out of bed.

He throws his school uniform on – picking it up from the floor.

He rushes downstairs and grabs a slice of toast as he leaves.

Tom walks slowly to school, often arriving late.

He struggles through the school day, making excuses for not doing homework as he goes.

At the end of the day he strolls back home and watches TV all evening.

How could Tom change his day? Suggest an 'enterprising' approach to Tom's day so that he has a better day at school. You could present your ideas in a table like the one below:

	An 'enterprising' approach to Tom's day
The night before:	• Do any homework required for the next day. • Arrange school uniform and schoolbooks for the next day. • Go to bed at a reasonable time.
The morning:	

Learning intentions

I am learning:

✓ to start a Personal Career Plan
✓ why it is important to start a Personal Career Plan.

In the last five topics you have been learning about different types of jobs, and that certain skills and qualities are needed in order to do different jobs well.

When you leave school, whether you go on to study further or not, you will eventually have opportunities to enter the world of work. As well as being a good match for your particular skills and qualities, the jobs or careers you eventually end up doing will depend on a number of other things, including:

- You the individual – your desires and wants, what influences and interests you.
- Your knowledge and understanding about different careers and jobs open to you.
- The local and global economy – which jobs are available locally and which you will have to move away to do.
- The changing nature of work – how developments in technology and globalisation are changing work.
- How you want to work and what options are available to you.

It is important to be aware of and learn about all of these in order to make the right choices. This is why you should start planning now. A good way to do this is to develop a Personal Career Plan (PCP), which you can revisit and update as often as you want.

A PCP is a process where you review all that you have achieved so far and then reflect on what you want to do and what you need to get there. It involves setting an ultimate goal and then listing the steps in order to achieve it. You may not yet know what your ultimate goal is, and that is why in the next few topics you will have the opportunity to do more research about the world of work and what influences you and interests you – and then have the opportunity to draw up some personal goals to go in your own PCP.

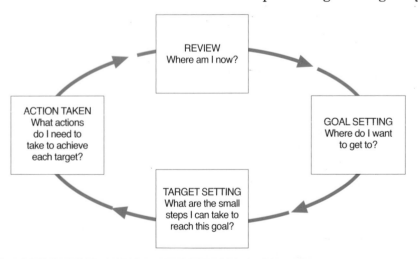

There are four steps in the Personal Career Planning Process as shown in the diagram.

There is no end to the process as once you reach a goal you should review and set a new goal.

Activity 1 New goals

As a class:

Discuss why you think it is important to keep setting new goals.

 # Activity 2 PCP model

Keira has just been given her Year 8 Christmas report. She has settled into her new school well but is disappointed with a few of her results. Keira's employability teacher suggests she goes through the PCP model to improve next term and Keira starts to fill in a PCP sheet as shown below.

a) In pairs:

- Make a copy of the PCP sheet below.
- Fill in the remaining actions for each of the targets.
- Add in one more target and the action for it.

b) Keira finishes just above average in her exam and achieves her goal, what do you think a goal for Year 9 could be?

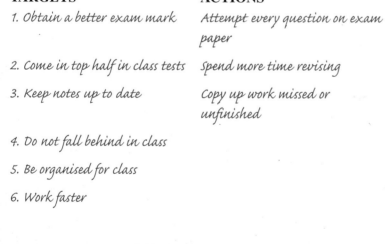

REVIEW I am – *below average in mathematics and disappointed.*

GOAL I want – *to finish above class average in the June mathematics exam.*

TARGETS	ACTIONS
1. Obtain a better exam mark	Attempt every question on exam paper
2. Come in top half in class tests	Spend more time revising
3. Keep notes up to date	Copy up work missed or unfinished
4. Do not fall behind in class	
5. Be organised for class	
6. Work faster	

Although, like Keira, you can use the PCP model to set goals at any time, before you can start your actual career plan you need to find out which type of career you are interested in. This will be the focus of the next eight topics. We will then go on to look at how to set goals and why this is important in a PCP.

Learning intentions

I am learning:

✓ to consider who or what actually influences career choices.

As we mentioned in topic 36, what interests and influences you will have an impact on the career or job you eventually choose. There are a number of factors that may influence you including:

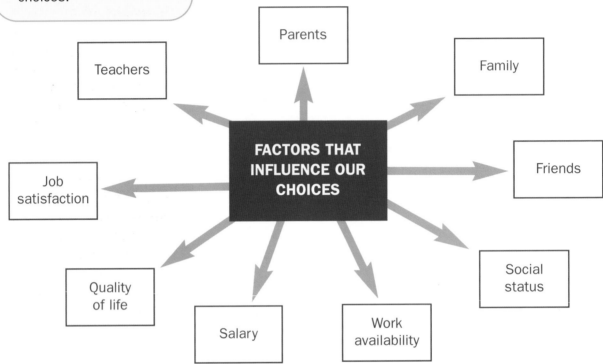

- Teachers
- Parents
- Family
- Job satisfaction
- **FACTORS THAT INFLUENCE OUR CHOICES**
- Friends
- Quality of life
- Salary
- Work availability
- Social status

Each factor will have a different amount of influence depending on what is most important to you. Take the singer-songwriter James Blunt for example. He started off a career as an army officer, as generations of his family had been in the army. However, he had been playing the guitar since the age of fourteen and eventually decided that music was where his real interest lay – and in 2006 he won two Brit Awards. So you can see how different influences affected both his career choices.

James Blunt

✓✗ Activity 1
Personal journal

Write in your journal what factors you think will be your main influences when thinking about a possible career. Give reasons for your choices.

Activity 2 What influences me?

This activity will require you to focus your thoughts on what influences you. Your school has produced a list of extra curricular activities. You must choose two from the list below.

Extra Curricular Activities	
Football or Rugby	Duke of Edinburgh Award Scheme
Hockey or Netball	Debating Society
School Choir	Art Club
School Drama Group	Craft Club
Scripture Union	Cross Country Running Club

a) Draw a table and write down the two activities you have chosen in two different columns.
b) Why have you picked those two? Underneath each activity explain the factors that you feel influenced your choice.
c) Feedback your choices to your class and explain why you want to take part in the extra curricular activities you have identified.

There are always good reasons for picking one activity against another; it is the same with jobs/careers.

There are a number of jobs which you may see each day, such as bus driver, teacher, shopkeeper, dinner supervisor, etc. You may have a good idea of what types of skills these jobs require and whether or not they interest you. However, there will be many different jobs that you don't know about. To find out about different jobs you can:
• ask your careers teacher
• ask your family
• carry out a job search on the internet.

 # Activity 3
Using the internet

a) Log on to the internet and do a search through a search engine, such as Google, for information about a job that interests you most. Or you could go to a specific careers website (see page 76 for some examples of these). Carry out your research in more depth, finding out information that you want/need to know.
b) As a class:
Discuss the different jobs that you have each identified, remembering to highlight the main factors that have influenced your choice.

 # Activity 4
Job influences

When you have completed activity 3, collect all the factors that have influenced you towards a particular job/career and present a montage on your classroom notice board. Each member of your class will do the same and when completed you and your class will have a visual picture of a wide range of jobs and the influencing factors that can be seen concerning those jobs/careers.

Education for Employability

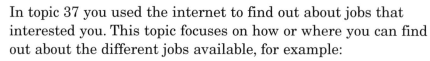

Learning intentions

I am learning:

✓ to find out how and where I can find information about different jobs

✓ to decide how useful different sources of careers information are.

In topic 37 you used the internet to find out about jobs that interested you. This topic focuses on how or where you can find out about the different jobs available, for example:

- careers advisors
- the internet
- talking to people in work
- newspapers.

Careers advisors

At school there is a careers advisor appointed by the Department of Education and Learning (DEL), who can give you advice on the different jobs and careers paths, and what you need to do in order to pursue them. Speak to your careers teacher to arrange an appointment.

The internet

The internet is becoming more and more useful both to find out about different types of jobs but also for employers to advertise vacant positions in their organisations. There are websites that act as a central place where employers can advertise such as:

- www.jobcentreonline.com
- www.loadzajobs.co.uk

On these sites you can find out about the requirements for different jobs which are currently available. There are also dedicated career advice websites such as:

- www.careers-gateway.co.uk

This website will give you a range of advice about different careers and links to other useful websites.

Activity 1 Information card

In groups:

a) Produce an information card that outlines details of a job you are all interested in, through researching it on the internet (a starting point would be the careers gateway website mentioned above). Your information card should include:

- A short history of the job, how long has it been around, has it changed since it was first available.
- A short description of what the job involves.
- The qualification needed for this particular job.
- The wages/salary that would be expected.
- How this job may change in the future.

b) Present your information card to the class.

c) As a class:
Vote on which four jobs you find the most interesting out of the ones that have been presented.

Talking to people in work

Another way of finding out about jobs, particularly those local to you, is talking to people in your family or other adults that you know that are in work. This will give extra 'insight' knowledge about the jobs they do (the good and the bad!) which you will usually not get from careers advisors, the internet or newspapers.

 ## Activity 2 Family and friends

a) Seek out someone close to you, it may be a relative or friend who is currently working or has just retired from work. Ask them:

- to talk to you about their work, what they do/did
- why they chose that career or job
- what changes have taken place in their job over the years
- would they recommend that particular line of work to you.

b) Report your findings to the class as a short speech.

Newspapers

Newspapers and job magazines are a good source of information about careers and jobs available. Some newspapers often focus on particular industries on different days of the week (for example the *Irish News* has public jobs on Thursdays and the *Belfast Telegraph* has general jobs on Fridays), and local newspapers advertise jobs in the local area. As well as advertising jobs, newspapers will also have information about what is happening in the economy and which companies are successful or going through hard times.

 ## Activity 3 Using newspapers and job magazines

a) Buy a local newspaper and research the current job market in your area. The *Belfast Telegraph* and the *Irish News* publishes information several times each week on jobs/careers. Find out the days that these are printed and what type of jobs they focus on.

b) Obtain the last copy of the jobs/careers printout from one of these two papers and highlight an article that is of special interest to you or your community.

c) Discuss with your class the advantages/disadvantages you have identified from carrying out this research in terms of how useful these papers are as sources of information about jobs. Are they more useful than the internet sites you have visited? Give reasons for your answers.

Learning intentions

I am learning:

✓ how to categorise jobs into different types

✓ about the range and variety of jobs in my local area

✓ to identify the employers in my local area.

In topic 38 you looked at different ways of identifying the different kinds of jobs that are available.

However, the jobs that you identified may no longer exist when you leave education.

In Northern Ireland the types of jobs which people do have changed over the past twenty years. For example, Ulster Carpets, a manufacturing company, reduced their workforce by over a third during 2005 and 2006, yet BT, who provide telecommunications services, are among Northern Ireland's top ten employers with over 3000 employees.

When you leave school, you may end up doing a job that didn't exist when your parents were leaving school! Certainly the jobs that are available to you now may not be the same as the options school leavers had twenty years ago. In later topics we will look at this changing nature of work, but in this topic you will learn how jobs can be categorised into different groups and identify some of the types of jobs currently available in your local area.

There are so many types of work that to start listing them all would take too long. We can however, organise jobs into main groups.

Activity 1 Get them sorted

The table below shows some of the main types of jobs.

a) Copy the table and add examples for each type from the jobs shown in the cartoons opposite.

b) As a class, brainstorm some local examples of jobs and employers for each type of job. Add these to your table. Can you fill in an example for each group?

Job type	Example from cartoon opposite	Local example/employer
Public Services and Care (emergency services, schools, government agencies)		
Animals or Plants		
Manufacturing (making things)		
Information and Communication Technology (ICT)		
Leisure, Travel and Tourism		
Retail (selling goods)		
Arts, Media and Publishing		
Finance		
Business Administration and Law		

Education for Employability

Solicitor

Accountant

Leisure centre attendant

Farmer

Firefighter

Television producer

Dressmaker

Plumber

Furniture delivery person

Software engineer

Activity 2 Job hunt

In order to do this activity you will need to have copies of the job finder section in the local paper from the last few weeks.

a) In groups:

Choose one of the job types from activity 1 – each group should choose a different type.

Use your copies of the local paper to identify adverts for jobs that belong to the job type you have chosen and list them.

b) As a class:

Construct a pictogram for your classroom wall, like the one which has been started below.

Use your pictogram as the basis of discussion for the following questions:

■ What type(s) of job is there a big demand for – why do you think this is?
■ What type(s) of job is there little or no demand for – why do you think this is?

Job Type	Number of jobs advertised
Animals or Plants	🐾🌳 🐾🌳 🐾🌳
Retail	🛍£ 🛍£ 🛍£ 🛍£ 🛍£
Leisure, Travel and Tourism	✈ ✈ ✈

KEY: Each symbol represents one job.

In topic 40 we shall look in more detail at why the types of jobs available in Northern Ireland are changing.

Education for Employability

Learning intentions

I am learning:

✓ to understand the reasons why some firms are moving out of Northern Ireland

✓ to investigate whether and why some jobs have disappeared from my local area.

Coats Barbour	Fighting Bull

In topic 39 you identified which jobs there are little or no demand for in your local area. If you had done this activity twenty years ago the picture may have been different – this is because changes take place in the local economy as employers move into and out of Northern Ireland. Two examples are given in the articles below and on page 81.

 Activity 1 Changes

Read through the news articles below and opposite, which are both true accounts.

In groups:

a) Draw a table with two columns, one headed Coats Barbour and the other Fighting Bull, like the one on the left. Discuss the two articles among your group and sort the information under each heading in your table to show:

■ Where is the company moving/expanding from and to?

■ What are the reasons for this move?

■ How will this affect the jobs available in Northern Ireland?

■ Does your group think this information has any implications for a Year 8 pupil's career plan?

b) Consider the case of Coats Barbour.

■ Discuss if you think the company in the article is right to move, think about it from the employees' point of view and also from the employers' or owners' point of view.

■ Have a class debate on this with some people in the class playing the managers and others the workers.

85 Jobs are axed at Coats Barbour

FOLLOWING months of speculation, Coats (UK) have announced they are to move production from Hilden (Lisburn), to its sites in Turkey and Hungary, with a loss of 85 jobs in the city … leading to the closure of the Hilden manufacturing site.

The Hilden site manufactures speciality threads for the automotive, upholstery and bedding industries.

The firm said that because the companies they are supplying have moved abroad it has 'made it essential' to move closer to them in order to keep their prices down and remain competitive.

'We have been compelled to restructure our business because of the industries we serve. The declining local market and the demand for lower costs from our customers means it is inevitable that we cannot continue to operate at Hilden. We must face the challenges of a highly competitive global market.'

The company has been one of Lisburn's best-known manufacturers for more than 170 years.

(Based on an extract from *Lisburn Echo* 01/02/06.)

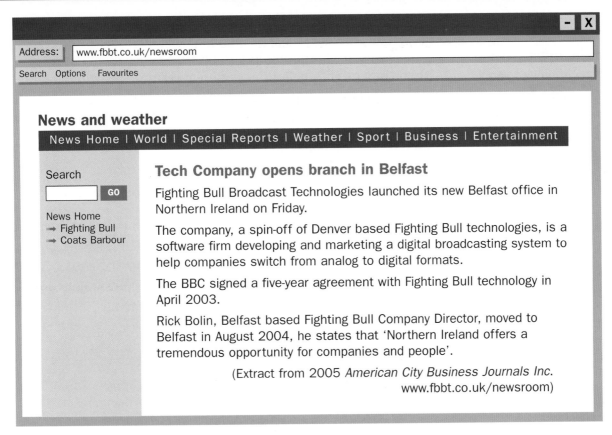

News and weather

News Home | World | Special Reports | Weather | Sport | Business | Entertainment

Search

[ ] GO

News Home
→ Fighting Bull
→ Coats Barbour

Tech Company opens branch in Belfast

Fighting Bull Broadcast Technologies launched its new Belfast office in Northern Ireland on Friday.

The company, a spin-off of Denver based Fighting Bull technologies, is a software firm developing and marketing a digital broadcasting system to help companies switch from analog to digital formats.

The BBC signed a five-year agreement with Fighting Bull technology in April 2003.

Rick Bolin, Belfast based Fighting Bull Company Director, moved to Belfast in August 2004, he states that 'Northern Ireland offers a tremendous opportunity for companies and people'.

(Extract from 2005 *American City Business Journals Inc.* www.fbbt.co.uk/newsroom)

Because of the high standard of education in Northern Ireland, companies are attracted here who need highly skilled workers, as in the ICT industry. Unfortunately, businesses which make things like clothing, carpets and fabrics are moving out of Northern Ireland.

 # Activity 2 What has changed?

What happened at Coats Barbour is typical of many manufacturing companies in Northern Ireland, the rest of Ireland and the UK.

a) Use the internet, local libraries, local history books and talk to grandparents or elderly friends to find an example of an employer near you that has either closed completely or become much smaller.

b) Be prepared to tell your classmates about:

- What the company does or did.
- Where they were based and how many they employed.
- How the company's situation has changed.
- A reason why you think this change has taken place.

In topic 41 you will examine another reason why the jobs now available in your area may have changed and continue to change.

Learning intentions

I am learning:

✓ how technology has changed our homes and lifestyles

✓ that technology is changing the workplace

✓ that changes in technology have meant changes in the types of jobs available.

In topic 40 we learned that the types of employment available in Northern Ireland are changing. Older manufacturing companies are becoming less important as local employers than they used to be and new employers are emerging as a result of changes in technology.

Developments in technology have had a huge impact on both life and work over the past 50 years – take the stories of Josh and Jim as an example.

 Activity 1 A day in the life of ...

a) Read Josh's and Jim's accounts and list the things in Josh's home that would not have been in Jim's.

b) In pairs:

■ Add to your list any other things you can think of that are in your home that would not have been in Jim's.

■ Discuss what differences the things on your list make to daily life.

Josh was 12 in 2006

My mum collects me from school most days in her car. When we get home I usually have a snack, sometimes I make hot chocolate in the microwave or on warm days I get a lolly from the freezer. My mum makes me do my homework next, which is pretty boring, but sometimes I get to go on the internet to find things out. Next is my free time! If it is dry I text my friend and we meet up for a game of football or to ride our bikes. If it is wet I play on my PlayStation or watch satellite TV. Before I know it, it is tea time – my favourite time of the day! After tea I have to help stack the dishwasher. I usually crash in front of a DVD for a while before I shower and get ready for bed. For supper my mum usually makes me a smoothie, she is really fussy about my five fruit and veg! Then I race up the stairs to get the electric toothbrush before my sister. Last of all I set my alarm clock, it's a really cool one and projects the time on to the ceiling.

Jim was 12 in 1956

I walk home from school each day; we do not have a car. At home I try to help my mum around the house. My main job is to clean out the fire and set it so that we will have hot water for washing clothes and dishes. If I have time I look for wood for the fire. After tea I play football outside or ride my bike. We are lucky as we are the only people in the street to have a telephone, and an inside toilet. Dad hopes to get mum something called a fridge, I think it is to keep our food fresh. Before I go to bed, dad lets us listen to the wireless and if there is bread left in the larder we toast it in front of the fire. I need to make sure my alarm clock is wound up each night as I help Billy deliver bread early in the morning.

In our homes many menial tasks have been replaced by modern devices, such as washing machines, which save a lot of time and physical work. Technology has also changed things in the workplace. In some cases this has meant certain jobs have disappeared and in other instances new jobs have been created. Some jobs no longer require people to carry them out at all – look at activity 2.

 Activity 2 Changing times

Look at the photographs below showing how technology has changed some workplaces. In pairs:

a) Compare each set of pictures and analyse how you think technology has impacted on the workplace shown.

b) Discuss how the jobs available may have changed.

c) Identify three jobs which you think are at risk of disappearing during the next twenty years because of changes in technology or lifestyle.

Changes in technology have had a massive impact on the jobs available. There will be jobs created by technology in the future that we may only be able to imagine now and you cannot assume that the job your grandfather did will still be required when you leave school. As part of your Personal Career Planning you need to stay informed about these changes. In topics 42 and 43 you shall look in more detail at the jobs available in your local area and why they may be changing.

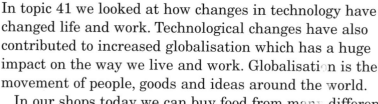

42 | WHAT ARE THE EFFECTS OF GLOBALISATION?

Learning intentions

I am learning:

✓ some examples of how globalisation has influenced life in Northern Ireland
✓ some reasons why globalisation has taken place
✓ reasons why people choose to work in different countries.

In topic 41 we looked at how changes in technology have changed life and work. Technological changes have also contributed to increased globalisation which has a huge impact on the way we live and work. Globalisation is the movement of people, goods and ideas around the world.

In our shops today we can buy food from many different countries, many of the clothes we wear reflect different cultures, the music from different countries is in our charts and we can find out what is happening around the world as it occurs. We can now access goods and ideas from around the world more easily than ever before.

This is globalisation – the world almost seems smaller.

 Activity 1 Global lives

a) Look at the images below of people in Northern Ireland. For each one identify how increased globalisation has had an impact on what they are doing/wearing.

b) In groups:

■ Look through some magazines and papers and identify pictures which show how globalisation has influenced the lifestyles of people in this country.

■ Cut out the most interesting pictures and make a collage to show the rest of your class. Be prepared to explain what each picture shows.

Globalisation has had a major impact, especially over the last twenty years. Life is very different for you growing up now than for your grandparents or even parents. You will have access to goods, ideas and opportunities in the workplace that they will not have had. What has happened to cause so many changes so quickly?

 ## Activity 2 Why globalisation?

As a class:

a) Brainstorm ideas about why globalisation has taken place. Here are a few words to prompt you:

■ communication ■ money ■ travel ■ EU ■ politics.

b) Think back to topic 41 on technology. Have developments in technology had a role to play in each of the ideas you have discussed?

In activity 2 you may have come up with the idea that globalisation has taken place because people can move about more freely than ever before and work in different countries. There are many people from different countries living and working in Northern Ireland and throughout the UK.

Quite often people do not end up working in the same place where they grow up, and globalisation has increased our opportunities to work abroad. Sometimes this is a choice that people have to make if the job they want is not available in their local area. Look at the example in activity 3.

 ## Activity 3 Meet Kris

Read Kris's story on the right.
In pairs:

a) Discuss the reasons Kris had for coming to Belfast and what the benefits to him have been. Do you think it was an easy decision for him?

b) Under the headings 'Advantages' and 'Disadvantages' make a list of reasons for and against leaving Northern Ireland to go and work somewhere else. Compare your list with another group.

Kris's story

I travelled over from Poland one year ago. I had to fly to England and then to Belfast. I had never flown before and was quite frightened. I came to Belfast because I had a friend already working in a restaurant here. Since coming to Belfast I have worked for a delivery firm, I work hard and they have given me more responsibility and more money.

In Poland I trained as a teacher, but the pay is very poor and I could not afford to do the things I wanted. I want to make money in the UK so that when I go home I can buy a house and get married. I have already made enough money to send home and pay for my father to have an operation. He is much better now.

Education for Employability

Learning intentions

I am learning:

✓ about the different patterns of work available

✓ why different work patterns suit different lifestyles.

As we learned in topic 42, globalisation has meant increased flexibility and opportunities to work outside your own locality. There are also other changes taking place in patterns of work which increase flexibility and which we shall look at in this topic.

During your school life you have to arrive and leave at certain times and you have to be on the premises. This used to be the case for workplaces but increasingly employers are offering people more options to fit in with their lifestyles. Below are just some of them.

Flexitime

Different employers have different models of flexitime but it usually allows employees to start and finish their work between certain times. For example, some have core working hours, e.g. 10a.m.–4p.m. when employees must be there but they can start and end when they want around these hours, e.g. 8–10a.m. start and 4–6p.m. finish. This means they can come in later if they need to or leave early and make the hours up another day. They will, however, need to work a set number of hours per month. In some companies if they work several long days they can even build up enough hours to take a day off!

Activity 1
Work to live

Read about the four people on page 87, who are each doing very different things in their life. In pairs:

a) Discuss each person's situation and choose a working pattern which would suit them better. What would the advantages of this be? How might it improve their lifestyle?

b) Choose one of the people you have looked at and prepare a role-play to present to your class, where one of you becomes the character and is interviewed by the other about their situation and how it has changed.

Teleworking

New technology means that some people can do their work from home. They use e-mail, fax machines and phone to keep in touch with others in the business.

Job sharing

This is when one full-time job is shared between two people. They split the hours of work, the amount of work, the pay and the holidays between them.

Career break

This is when your employer agrees to give you a period of time off work, usually one to two years. You do not get paid but your job will still be there when you return.

What sort of people would want to work like this?

Jane has three children all under the age of seven. She starts every day at 6.30a.m. so that she can get the baby to day nursery and the older children to friends' houses to be taken to school. Today she has to ask her boss to let her go at 4.15p.m. as her daughter's teacher wants to speak to her. She knows her boss will not be pleased as she is supposed to stay until 5.00p.m. Jane likes her job and she needs the money.

Ryan always wanted to be an accountant and the pay is good. However, sometimes he feels he is missing out on something. He wants to travel and experience more of life before he really settles down. But this is a great firm and he doesn't want to give up such a good job.

Joe feels he can't do anything right. He is under stress at work because he feels he wants to be with his wife more. Although he doesn't really need to work any more he loves his job. He feels guilty about not being at home and guilty about not giving his best in his job.

Anna's architects firm have recently moved offices. She now has to travel much further. This means a very early start for her whole family and she is spending a lot more on petrol. She has considered moving house but that would mean moving schools. Anna normally works alone or leaves the office to travel to meet clients.

For many of you your first experience of the world of work may come from part-time or seasonal work while you are still in full-time education. This can be extremely useful in developing many of the skills and qualities discussed in topics 32–34. Seasonal work is when people are employed to do jobs which may only be required at certain times of the year. The photos on the right show two obvious examples.

Activity 2
Seasons change

As a class:
Brainstorm examples of seasonal work in your local area.

Learning intentions

I am learning:

✓ how to set my own personal goals

✓ how to measure success

✓ how to break down goals into smaller steps.

Throughout this section on Education for Employability you have been learning about some of the different factors that you need to take into account when deciding what job you would like to do. When you decide on what you would like to do in the future, it is important to set goals in order to achieve what you set out to do. This topic looks at how you can set goals to develop your Personal Career Plan.

Since your birth the government has set goals for you, for example at seven months old you were expected to sit upright on your own. In the activity below you will think about some other goals set for you.

 ## Activity 1 Timeline

Draw a line down the side of a page with 0–18 years scaled on it as shown on the left.

a) Using the statements below place each beside the correct age in the diagram to show some of the goals set for you that you have reached or will reach in the next seven years.

■ Start school ■ Start post-primary school ■ Sit GCSE exams
■ Sit KS3 exams ■ Leave school

b) Can you add any other goals that have been set for you to the timeline?

From a young age you will also have been setting yourself personal goals. For example you may have wanted:

• to ride a bicycle without stabilisers
• to be good at a certain game
• to be liked by your close friends.

When you achieved each of these goals you will have felt a sense of achievement. But how did you measure the success of achieving them?

For example in the above goals success could be measured by:

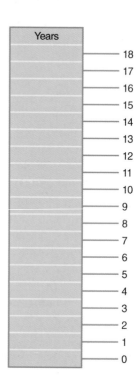

Years
18
17
16
15
14
13
12
11
10
9
8
7
6
5
4
3
2
1
0

Being able to cycle unaided for 10 metres.

Gaining a place on a team playing that game.

Having people confide in you and keep your secrets.

Success will mean different things to different people, we all look at success in a different way and inwardly we know if we have been successful at a certain thing or not.

Being smart

We should all set ourselves personal goals that are achievable. We all want to be successful in something. A useful way of successfully reaching our goals is to be SMART when we are setting them. That is:

Specific   – what exactly will you do?
Manageable   – have you the time and resources to carry it out?
Achievable   – how will you know you have achieved this step?
Realistic   – remember to consider your abilities.
Time   – when do you hope to finish each target and reach your goal?

 Activity 2 Achieving goals

a) Individually:

- Think of three goals you have had in the past. Write these down and under each one write the letters SMART.
- Now consider what a SMART goal means, put a tick or cross beside each letter to indicate if your goal was: Specific, Manageable, Achievable, Realistic or had Time to reach it.

b) As a class:

- Discuss how it feels when you achieve your goal.
- How does it feel when you fail to reach a goal or cannot say for certain if you were successful?
- Why do you think having a time for each target is important?

As shown in topic 36, the path towards reaching a goal is made up of lots of smaller steps, called targets, and the actions needed to get there.

Over the next five years you will make some important choices about a future career path. Your goal will be to decide what you want to do when you are sixteen. This decision will be easier if you break it down into smaller steps, see activity 3.

 **Activity 3**
Personal journal

Write down what you want to do when you reach the end of Year 12.

Draw a flow chart showing the targets and actions you can take to reach this goal.

The targets should be in order starting with what you need to do first at the bottom. An example has been given below.

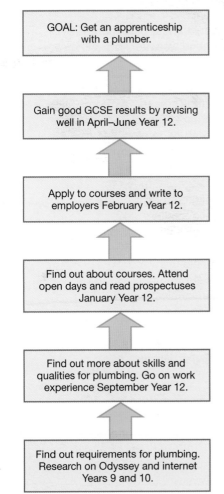

GOAL: Get an apprenticeship with a plumber.

Gain good GCSE results by revising well in April–June Year 12.

Apply to courses and write to employers February Year 12.

Find out about courses. Attend open days and read prospectuses January Year 12.

Find out more about skills and qualities for plumbing. Go on work experience September Year 12.

Find out requirements for plumbing. Research on Odyssey and internet Years 9 and 10.

You have now taken your first steps in developing your Personal Career Plan. In book 2 and throughout Year 9, you will start to use the information you have learned so far and think about what it means for you and your choices over the next few years.

INDEX

Index